AUG 2 7 2019

MW00446945

Brimming with creative inspiration, how-to projects, and useful information to enrich your everyday life, Quarto Knows is a favorite destination for those pursuing their interests and passions. Visit our site and dig deeper with our books into your area of interest: Quarto Creates, Quarto Cooks, Quarto Homes, Quarto Lives, Quarto Drives, Quarto Explores, Quarto Gifts, or Quarto Kids.

Inspiring | Educating | Creating | Entertaining

First published in 2018 by Motorbooks, an imprint of The Quarto Group, 100 Cummings Center, Suite 265-D, Beverly, MA 01915, USA. T (978) 282-9590 F (978) 283-2742 QuartoKnows.com

Motorbooks titles are also available at discount for retail, wholesale, promotional, and bulk purchase. For details, contact the Special Sales Manager by email at specialsales@quarto.com or by mail at The Quarto Group, Attn: Special Sales Manager, 100 Cummings Center, Suite 265-D, Beverly, MA 01915, USA.

10 9 8 7 6 5 4 3 2

ISBN: 978-0-7603-5359-2
Library of Congress Cataloging-in-Publication Data

Names: Brutt, Ryan, 1983- author.
Title: Muscle car barn finds : rusty Road Runners, abandoned AMXs, crusty
   Camaros and more! / by Ryan Brutt.
Description: Minneapolis, Minnesota : Motorbooks, [2017]
Identifiers: LCCN 2017029798| ISBN 9780760353592 (hc w/jacket) | ISBN
   9780760359785 (eISBN)
Subjects: LCSH: Muscle cars--Collectors and collecting--United
   States--Anecdotes. | Brutt, Ryan, 1983---Travel--United States--Anecdotes.
Classification: LCC TL23 .B73 2018 | DDC 629.2220973--dc23
LC record available at https://lccn.loc.gov/2017029798

Acquiring Editor: Zack Miller
Project Manager: Jordan Wiklund
Art Director: James Kegley
Layout: Simon Larkin

Printed in China

MUSCLE CAR CAR *Barn Finds*

Rusty Road Runners, Abandoned AMXs, Crusty Camaros and More!

RYAN BRUTT

motorbooks

DEDICATION

I would like to dedicate this book to my family, friends, and fans, especially my mother. Without their love, support, and leads over these many years, I wouldn't be where I am today. Thank you.

CONTENTS

INTRODUCTION

It's always difficult for me to do these introductions. I am not one to talk about myself; I usually talk about the adventures I've been on and the cars I've found, not really about myself as a person. It's really not all that interesting, but it's what I do that is interesting: Driving around the country documenting cool cars in neglected situations. Here's a small peek into my world and the way I evolved into The Auto Archaeologist.

You'd think I was a hardcore car guy from the start, but it couldn't be further from the truth. I was into trains as a child, but as a teenager, I considered cars as only a mode of transportation. My father used to tell me about the last new car he bought, a 1970 Hemi 'Cuda. I knew it was cool, but it really didn't sink in until a trip to a radio installation shop in Chicago.

It is not very often that a person can trace their passion back to a single event or car, but I'm lucky in that regard. The radio in my first car—a 1990 Ford Taurus Wagon—had died, and my father had

Not the normal use of a Gremlin, but it does the job well, protecting the Javelin AMX sitting up top in Michigan.

Next to the regular Burnt Orange Challenger was the owner's other car, a 1970 Dodge Challenger T/A. This one sat at the Packard Plant in storage until the place was condemned and he was able to bring the vehicle home.

arranged to get a new one installed at a friend's shop. It would take hours, and before smart phones and such, I got bored and began walking around. Between the two main work areas of the shop was a black car, buried in junk. I unburied the car a bit and saw it had a really nice shape to it; it had "gills" on the fenders, and the grille looked like it was going to eat you. And that's when I saw the badge on the back: 'Cuda. It turned out to be a 1971 Plymouth 'Cuda. This thing was just so cool, with the chrome and angry look. And here it was just sitting there, buried in the shop. People walked past it every day and never paid it any attention. If this car was just sitting in a shop in Chicago and I found it by accident, what other cool cars were still out there? If I started looking for them, what could I turn up?

That started it all. On weekends I would head out with friends, combing the countryside looking for old cars. We'd always find something interesting, and just like the '71 'Cuda, they were never for sale. So I just kept at it, getting deeper and deeper into the muscle car world. I took every opportunity to talk to people and follow up on leads. Some were duds, but others revealed incredible cars in amazing situations.

I always told people, I'm here for the story, not the car. The car has been sitting for 20, 30, 40, or 50 years, so obviously it isn't for sale. But why has the car been sitting that long, and what connection do you have to it that you never let the car go? There must be a good story for you to let them sit so long. And more than likely, the owners are more than happy to talk to someone about the car—someone who isn't trying to take it from them. It has allowed me the opportunity to see some amazingly rare cars sitting in sad locations.

In the end, I always leave my business card in the glove box. I'm more than happy to help an individual out, and if the car comes up for sale, I can try to purchase it, or I can get them in touch with individuals who are straight shooters and won't lowball them. Or, if they ever want it restored, I can point the owners in the right direction of good, quality shops. The option used most often, I'm pleased to say, is the owners call asking where to find parts for the cars because they do want to get them going again. Sometimes my enthusiasm rubs off on them, and they want to get it going, or they just want to hear it run again. Either way, the car won't be sitting anymore.

Before I was writing in car magazines, I had (still have) a blog about my adventures. I documented the cars with my little digital camera, then did write-ups about the adventures, and posted the pictures. It became popular enough that I made friends in the automotive journalist world. I did some freelance work for magazines such as *Mopar Collector's Guide* and *Mopar Muscle*. One day I got a message from David Freiburger, the head editor of *Hot Rod* Magazine. He mentioned that they were doing a big refresh of the magazine and wondered if I would be interested in doing a monthly column for the magazine. Everything from there on is history. I've had a monthly column in *Hot Rod* now for years, and have been able to have work featured in a variety of magazines.

This newfound, very public profile led me to create my other personal website, The Auto Archaeologist. That way I could keep my regular life private, but post all my cool car adventures. This was a major boon to my collection of clues and leads. Normally, I had them all in a spreadsheet on my computer, organized by state, by zip code, and so forth, so I had a general idea of where things were when traveling. That all changed when I found Google My Maps. This allows you to have a private map online you can pin locations to. And not just pin a location, but you can enter comments and notes and more. So I was able to plot out every lead and every story on a map. Since it was in Google, I could see while traveling which pins I was near, giving me the ability to hit up a bunch of finds every trip. It revolutionized the way I find barn finds.

That's the gist of how I started and how I operate. Anyone can do it, it just takes a little time and a little effort. People say all the time that there are no more cool cars to be found. And I am out there proving them wrong every time.

A side note about the 1971 'Cuda that was my big epiphany car: I went back to that shop recently and learned the car had disappeared shortly after I had seen it about 15 years earlier. After talking to

Walking through a junkyard in the spring, this jumped out at me as a surprise: an early C3 Corvette languishing in the yard. It was an original 454 car to boot!

the owner of the shop about how that car changed my world, he invited me back into the shop, where that exact car was back in the exact same spot! But it had been fully restored and was in the final assembly! It blew my mind. And there, sitting on another car, I saw it: the original grille for the car. It had some cracks and was missing some parts, so they got a new one. And as a gift, he sold me the grille for next to nothing. So I now own the exact grille from the exact car that changed my life. When he did that, it made me the happiest man in the world. It just took 15 years!

THE AERO W

RACE ON SUNDAY AND SELL on Monday. That was the motto for the major car manufacturers for decades. The cars you could see running around in NASCAR could be bought right off your local dealership sales floor. And it worked. As in the name indicated—National Association for Stock Car Auto Racing—they were "stock" cars equipped with safety equipment and raced around the track.

You could say NASCAR started well before the sanctioning body came into effect, and that it started with bootleggers seeing which of their moonshine runners was faster. It quickly evolved from there into NASCAR, and as the years went on, more and more advancements were made in the development and design of cars for the series. Every season, things got more and more fine-tuned, with cars getting lower, with bigger engines. It was a very slippery slope.

Into the 1960s Dodge/Plymouth and Ford/Mercury had it out for one another. Dodge/Plymouth had given a black eye to the other race teams in 1964 with the debut of the new 426 Hemi in its race cars at the Daytona 500. These cars went on to finish 1-2-3-4 in the race. NASCAR developed strict rule changes to keep the Hemi in check, but they were later loosened. Still, the gauntlet had been dropped, and from there on, it was a race to best NASCAR vehicle.

In 1969, Ford had developed the Talladega, which was based on the Torino/Fairlane at the time in response to the news that Dodge was making a new, more aerodynamic Dodge Charger

Famous for sitting in Stephens Performance for decades, this Daytona was resurrected shortly after these pictures were taken.

ARRIORS

DAYTONA

11

called the 500. The Ford was named for the Talladega Superspeedway in Alabama that had opened up that same year. Ford used the "SportsRoof" option for better aerodynamics, but up front the cars originally had a recessed grille that looked good but created horrible airflow problems. So a more aerodynamic nose was put on the car, and it had a flush-mounted grille so air flowed over the car with much less turbulence. The rocker panels were rolled in, so the car could sit lower and look fairly stock. Another trick was to cut a rear bumper to make it a bit narrower, and give it a slight "V" shape. That helped create better downforce, much like an air dam is used now.

NASCAR rules required that 500 units of a model had to be produced for the public to purchase; otherwise the model could not be raced. To make these units as cheaply as possible, Ford built all the cars with the same engine, a 428 Cobra Jet V-8 with a C6 automatic transmission and bench seats. It is said that Ford still lost money on every car sold. Roughly 754 Talladegas were produced. Plymouth at the time was not producing an aerodynamic car that could compete with the Talladega, so Richard Petty, one of the all-time best drivers in NASCAR, switched to Ford for one season, and he won his 100th race in his Talladega.

OPPOSITE TOP: This was jokingly referred to as the "parts car" Superbird by the owner, but that can't be further from the truth. It has been sitting while he works on his other three Superbirds.

OPPOSITE BOTTOM: You won't believe it unless you see it: an original 1970 Superbird in a large lean-to with a large chain around the wing to help keep it safe.

BELOW: Here sits a 1969 Dodge Daytona, an original family car. I see this car once a year, and it has never moved in the many years I've gone by.

Mercury did nearly the same thing with its NASCAR vehicle, the Cyclone, adding a more aerodynamic front nose with a flush-mounted grille. The bumpers and rockers were designed like those of the Talladega, as the Talladega design was basically copied on the Cyclones. This worked very well and made the Cyclones extremely competitive. The productions units were a bit different, though, as they all had the 351 Windsor V-8, the C6 automatic, and a front bench seat.

Dodge led the charge for Mopar. The new-for-1968 Charger looked awesome, but serious aerodynamic flaws, such as the large, recessed grille and sunken rear window area, made it uncompetitive in NASCAR. The 1969 model year's standard Charger did not help matters, so a plan was hatched. To go faster than everyone else, the Hemi would either need a big boost in power, which was unfeasible, or the car needed to pass through the air easier. The second option was much easier and cheaper, so the 1969 Dodge Charger 500 was developed.

The Charger 500 had a flush-mounted grille that was taken from 1968 Dodge Coronet, and the rear window area was made into a fastback style. It looked the part of a fast car, but unfortunately, it did not perform as well as hoped. The 500 production cars came with either a 440 or 426 Hemi, a four-speed or automatic, and a variety of other options. It just wasn't slippery enough for the racetrack, so Dodge went back to the drawing board and developed the Daytona.

The Daytona was just about the wildest vehicle an American auto manufacturer had ever produced. It looked like nothing else on the road. After months of testing in wind tunnels, the designers popped out the 1969 Dodge Charger Daytona, named for the Daytona International Superspeedway in Florida. It had a large, peaked nose up front; a large wing at the rear; and it retained the fastback rear window of the 500. And it rocked. It was fast and did very well in NASCAR. It didn't win the title, but it was right there.

Plymouth didn't do anything aerodynamic with its cars for the most part, until they lost Richard Petty to Ford. The 1970 Road Runners underwent wind tunnel testing and another wonder was produced: the 1970 Plymouth Superbird. (Get it? Superbird—based on the Road Runner.) It was enough to lure Petty back to Plymouth and he won the 1970 NASCAR title in a Superbird.

It cost Plymouth, though. Because of these crazy cars Ford and Mopar were producing, NASCAR boosted the homologation

OPPOSITE TOP LEFT: Walking up to this car, you would think this 1970 Superbird had been sitting for decades, but it had only been put into storage for a short time. But little room makes the car a shelf in winter!

OPPOSITE TOP RIGHT: The car in the next bay was a different story. This is a 1969 Dodge Charger 500 that had been sitting for many years and took a bit of work to unbury the nose enough to snap these pics.

OPPOSITE INSET (LEFT TO RGIHT): The Superbird, which got turned around since I saw it last, is a 440 six-barrel car with a four-speed.

This Mercury Cyclone Spoiler hasn't moved much in the few years I've known it, but it wouldn't need much to get it up and going.

Another one of the 500 owner's cars, this Ford Talladega was moved from a tight barn spot to a more easily accessible location.

Unburied from where it once sat, this 1969 Charger 500 moved from one side of the barn to another in the time that I've known about it. The owner has one of every Aero Warrior model.

BELOW: Here you can see what happens when the garage burns the aircraft-grade aluminum wing off a 1970 Superbird; only the ends survived.

requirements from 500 to over 1,000 units for public consumption. Plymouth produced roughly 1,935 cars, and lost money on every one. While the Daytonas and 500s sold fairly well, some Superbirds sat on dealers' lots for years before they were offloaded for a song.

Sadly, time marches on. With new, more-stringent rules coming down from NASCAR, the Hemi and other big engines were out after 1971. Ford was already out in 1970 because of the new rules. So by 1971, there were few aero warriors on NASCAR tracks. But their legacy has never been forgotten, and their rarity has made those Aero Warriors some of the most expensive muscle cars in the world!

FOR MANY YEARS BEFORE I started seriously getting into barn finds and hidden gems, there was a picture circulating in the Mopar web forums of a bunch of cool cars, including two Superbirds, tucked away in a storage building of some kind. It always had my interest, and every time it popped up online, I would ask about it to see if anyone knew who owned the cars. Nobody ever responded. Years passed, and while I remembered the picture, not many other pictures existed with a collection of cars quite like that! Then one day I got a message from a gentleman saying that if I were ever passing through Pennsylvania, to drop him a line. He had a few cool cars stashed that I would probably appreciate seeing. I put the guy's information on my map for a future adventure, and then forgot about it.

Eventually, I was heading in the gentleman's direction, so I sent him an email letting him know I would be in his neck of the woods and was still interested in taking a look at his collection. We set up a time to meet up, and a few weeks later I traveled east to Pennsylvania, a place I had only driven through once before. It was quite beautiful and surprisingly very hilly. Being from

This 1969 Dodge Daytona sits quietly behind a fake wall in an auto parts store in Pennsylvania. This car has been fully restored, but has been sitting for year, and to get it out from its hiding spot would require either going through a wall or moving several tons of equipment.

CHAPTER 1

Chicago, I wasn't used to driving twisty roads, but I made it to the location without incident.

This was definitely an old-school area, an agricultural part of the country. The car owner's store was an auto parts store looking like so many other small town auto parts stores. I walked in and was immediately back in my days at NAPA in DeKalb, Illinois. At the back of the store, at the parts counter with staffers on the phone or helping customers with their parts needs, I waited my turn.

I introduced myself to the car owner. He was about my height, but leaner. He told me the business had been his father's and was now his. He told me to follow him, that he had a surprise for me, and he was absolutely right—it was a surprise!

We walked to another part of the building that used to be a small engine shop. We came around the corner of a false store wall and what I saw blew my mind. There was a 1969 Dodge

Charger Daytona and more. There were two 1967 Hemi Plymouth GTXs and a 1969 Dodge Superbee Six Pack.

I've had many surprises in my travels, but this was right up there near the best of all time. The building's false wall made it possible to hide the cars, and nobody would be the wiser. It was an ingenious way to keep the cars close, but there was the issue of how to get them out of this space. The cars would have to go down a hallway at the back of the building, a hallway clogged with merchandise and machinery. To get them out would be a serious chore. Hypothetically, he said, if something was to happen and they had to get the cars out quickly, they would just run them through the side wall!

There weren't just cars in this mystery space, but there were also oh so wonderful parts. Spare 1970 Plymouth Superbird noses? There were three! Need a Shaker Hood for a 1970 Plymouth 'Cuda? That was there as well—and this was just the first level. We made our way into the storage basement where there were some of the most amazingly rare parts, neatly stacked and organized on shelves. There were 426 Hemi heads, spare steering columns for all manner of Mopars, rims, intakes for all major Mopar engines such as the 426 Hemi, 440, 340, etc. He didn't discriminate. And everything was organized and labeled. I was truly walking through a muscle car wonderland. And there was more.

We made our way to an old storage building of his elsewhere in town. It was truly old school, with the lower of the two stories built

OPPOSITE TOP: Acquired in a deal for three 1970 Plymouth Superbirds, this 1970 Superbird has been sitting in this spot for decades. It's the same spot from the famous picture that I remember seeing online years ago that inspired me to go find cool cars in barns.

OPPOSITE INSET: Here is the same 1970 Superbird from a side where you can more clearly see the extra original Superbird nose, and mismatched door. This one is fairly complete with the original 440-cubic-inch V-8 still sitting between the front fenders.

RIGHT: Tucked away in another storage building away from the other orange car, this is the third 1970 Superbird from the deal (another one was sold off recently). This one has been completely blasted apart to fix rust and other issues with the body, but you can still see the holes in the rear quarter panels where the wing would bolt into place.

into a hill, almost like a basement. We started on the top floor where, in a center storage area were two very nicely restored cars, a 1970 Hemi Plymouth Road Runner and a 1970 Plymouth 'Cuda 440 Six Barrel. Both had only been sitting a short time, and looked to be in perfect condition. But it was what I saw next door that really brought the whole experience home: It was THE spot from the picture that had captivated me for years.

In the photo, three Superbirds were tucked into a corner of the room, and a variety of rare Mopars filled the rest filled of the space. Unfortunately, the scene had changed slightly in the decade or so since the picture was taken—but not by much. There was still a single Superbird left in the room, and a 1970 'Cuda. It was incredible to me to be able to touch a piece of my personal history. This place had haunted my dreams.

Below us was the cherry topping the cake. We walked down to the lower level and the place was filled with muscle cars. Most of them were Dodges and Plymouths, and the third Superbird from the epic photo was stored down there. It was in pieces, and was nothing but a shell. But it was the final piece of the puzzle. You could see the holes in the quarters where the wing had been mounted, and large "PLYMOUTH" decals on the quarter panels. There was no mistaking what it was.

Exploring these locations had been quite the experience, to say the least. The cars and their quality and rarity are almost beyond description. I felt fortunate enough to get the opportunity to document them with the owner, and to tell their story.

Can't miss the wing on an original 1970 Superbird. This is the same car as before. The wing was unique to the Superbird and it was part of the homologation needed to run the cars in NASCAR. The wings are made from aircraft-grade aluminum because of the tremendous air pressures the wings are subjected to at high speeds.

THERE ARE STASHES OF RARE, desirable cars out there that you hear of, but simply cannot fathom. You can't believe cars of this high quality are just sitting there, possibly unappreciated or undiscovered. It's almost like trying to find a lost civilization: You've heard stories it exists, but haven't laid eyes on it. Thankfully I was able to change all that.

Many years ago, I saw a few pictures online of a warehouse where a decent number were stashed. That's not out of the ordinary; there are countless barns and warehouses around the country full of cars. They're most commonly ordinary old cars, nothing particularly rare. But this was not one of those places. This stash contained an impressive quantity of Aero Warriors, not just one or two, but nearly 20 cars in varied conditions. And the photos showed they were properly stored in a warehouse on a concrete floor, not just a metal shed in the middle of nowhere. But that was all that the post contained, just a few photos and little explanation of the cars shown.

I thought of those photos often, and I'd hear stories about them, but nobody knew exactly where the stash was—until I was at the Wellborn Muscle Car Museum. A gentleman there had seen the collection and knew exactly where it was. Luck had it that I could visit the

From this angle, the abuse this Superbird endured is clearly seen. The paint on the wing had been baked away by the sun, and some of the owner's efforts to restore it can be seen.

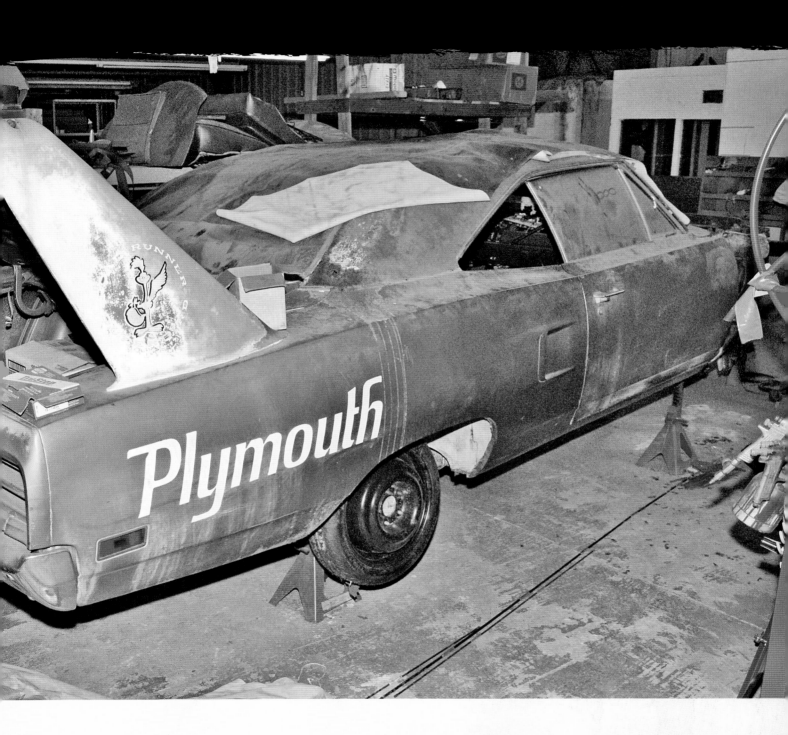

ABOVE: Walking into a large warehouse in Tennessee, it is hard to believe that so much incredible history is under the roof. This 1970 Plymouth Superbird is in the process of being restored back to its original luster.

MIDDLE LEFT: A rougher 1970 Superbird, in the same color as the first one but never in such good shape as long as this owner had it. It needs a lot of work, including a lot of metalwork. Thankfully, it is no longer rusting away outside and is in a nice, dry warehouse in the meantime.

MIDDLE RIGHT: A better view of the metalwork that needs to go on with this poor Superbird. The quarter is still with the car, at least, sitting there in the open trunk. You can clearly see the holes in the fender where the wing bolts into place.

BOTTOM LEFT: Here is another 1970 Superbird currently under restoration. The nosecone had just been liberated from the front of the car and the 440-cubic-inch V-8 had been rebuilt. This one had been sitting for a prolonged period of time, but even with all sitting, it is still fairly solid.

BOTTOM RIGHT: Here is a good view of the condition of the same Superbird. It is by no means perfect, but it is in pretty good shape for sitting for so long. You can see in the trunk the special brackets Plymouth used to keep the large wings in place. The brackets bolted to the wings from the inside of the car and to the frame rails at the other end.

INSET (LEFT TO RIGHT): Sitting for so long that mold had been growing on the exterior, this 1969 Talladega has seen better days, but it was rescued from a horrible existence by the warehouse owner, and with a little bit of work (and maybe a car wash), it could easily be reborn.

Tucked away in another part of the warehouse, a fairly rough 1969 Mercury Cyclone Spoiler sits neglected. This is another project that the owner rescued. It looks as though someone started a restoration and just gave up. It is now safely secure in the warehouse.

For a Ford, this is one of the rarest cars you can find. This original 1969 Ford Talladega was rescued from a field. The current owner heard it was going to be destroyed and rescued it, putting it in his warehouse.

BELOW: This is one of my favorite cars in this collection. It is a nearly all-original 1970 Superbird with dog dish center caps, black steel wheels, a 440-cubic-inch V-8 with a four-barrel carburetor, and a four-speed manual transmission. I personally would drive the car as is because it has such a great look to it.

location on my way home, with only a slight detour, so I headed north from the museum to see this legendary place in person.

I reached the collection's owner by phone and he agreed to meet to show me the cars. Mike, the owner, said his father used to have a car leasing and sales company in town. Mike was in school and entering the car business with his father just as the Aero Warriors were emerging in NASCAR racing. Working with Ford training program, Mike got an internship at Holman-Moody, the legendary shop that set up all of Ford's NASCAR race cars. And seeds of the collection were sown.

He started saving these cars he loved. Ford Talladegas, Mercury Cyclone Spoilers, Superbirds, even a Charger Daytona and a Charger 500. His father's company had a large storage building near their main shop where Mike could stash the cars. He didn't

ABOVE: Here's something you would not expect to see: the rusted, burned-up hull of an original Superbird. This one had been used for circle-track racing, and it was beaten and abused. It had been relegated to a farm field and was about to be crushed when the warehouse owner rescued it.

OPPOSITE BOTTOM: The engine that came out of the burned-up Superbird was a bit different. An original 426 Hemi, one of the most desirable engines ever produced, this one is still fairly complete for sitting for so long. It has been rescued and is currently being rebuilt!

simply put them away—he restored them and has been recognized for his great work.

As Mike and I headed to the warehouse where the cars were stored, its plain exterior gave no hint at the precious cargo inside. We entered in the dark as a thunderstorm raged, but with the lights turned on, the hidden treasures were on full view. Here was a pair of perfectly restored, rare Ford Talladegas and a Dan Gurney Special Mercury Cyclone Spoiler. In front of me was a Dodge Charger Daytona, and next to that was a Charger 500. And this was all visible on first glance!

The Daytona was a work in progress, with all the bodywork done and work on the engine and interior underway, but the Fords and the Mercury were in near-perfect condition. The Charger 500 had been sitting a while, but was clean and looked like it could be running again with only a bit of work.

The warehouse was divided into multiple large, open areas separated by large doors that made it easy to move the cars about. In the next area we entered was another Mercury Cyclone that needed a bit of work, along with a blue 1970 Superbird that was his daughter's car and in the midst of being restored. They had just finished rebuilding the car's original 440-cubic-inch V-8, so the project was moving right along, and this car had a great patina to it. The decals on the quarters had just the right look, one that can't be duplicated.

Elsewhere in the warehouse was a rusted-out husk of a car. Some people would have scrapped the car and moved on. But Mike knew it was an original 1970 Superbird with many of the rare Superbird components still in place. Apparently, the car was used in some circle-track racing, then was involved in a fire and left in a field to rust away. It was later going to be crushed, but Mike stepped in and saved it. It was no candidate for restoration, but Mike expected to find some way to display it.

Through another door were several large benches and engines on stands, including a complete 426-cubic-inch Hemi V-8. Just over 10,000 street Hemi cars were produced between 1966 and 1971, and I was told this was a 1970 Hemi, a true rarity, and a welcome surprise.

OPPOSITE TOP: Surprisingly, this is the only 1969 Dodge Charger 500 the owner has, originally a green car with a green interior and a 440-cubic-inch V-8. This one is pretty close to being finished. It has just been sitting while other projects with greater needs get put ahead of it.

OPPOSITE INSET LEFT Another 1969 Cyclone sits in a line of saved cars, this one having been sitting for a long time even before it was rescued and put in the warehouse. For sitting so long, the car is actually in pretty good shape, so it waits its turn to get going again.

OPPOSITE INSET RIGHT: A better view of the unique front end of this Cyclone Spoiler. It had been sitting outside for so long, the original stripes have faded away into almost nothing. And the original 351-cubic-inch V-8 is nowhere to be found.

BELOW: My favorite 1969 Talladega in the group was this blue one, mostly original, except with lots of mold and moss growing on the exterior. Wherever this car once sat was not warm and dry. Thankfully, it was rescued and with a good wash will probably look great again.

Near the Hemi was what I'm more used to, but not in such numbers. There were two rows of rusty, crusty Ford Talladegas, Mercury Cyclones, and a Superbird, all of them cars Mike had rescued from farm fields or junkyards. The rarest of the bunch was the Superbird. Most of the rescue cars were complete and looked like they could be running again with just a bit of work.

As we continued our explorations, I saw two more Superbirds, one which was Mike's main project, a blue '70 Superbird that he used to display at shows. The other Superbird was not as nice since at some point, someone had cut the quarter off the car and it was missing

ABOVE: One of the worst in the bunch, this 1969 Talladega was missing a lot of parts. Someone at some point had started trying to restore it, but stopped. Thankfully, it is in the right place to be put back together properly.

INSET RIGHT: This poor 1969 Talladega did not lead a very healthy life. A kid put the car into a pole and then the car sat for decades. Knowing what the car was, and not wanting it to be neglected any more than it already had, Mike rescued it.

OPPOSITE TOP: I see a trend as another 1969 Talladega sits in the warehouse. It was purchased years ago, tucked away, and doesn't need a lot of restoration. The original 428 and transmission still sit under the hood.

OPPOSITE MIDDLE: Talladega is one of the cleaner cars that were rescued. It looks as though it was simply driven into the garage and parked.

OPPOSITE BOTTOM: Another forlorn 1969 Talladega sits in a row of other rescued vehicles. This car was rescued from either being sent to the junkyard or crushed. It is a complete car and not in horrible condition. So it sits in the back of the warehouse until the time is right.

parts. Of all of Mike's Superbirds, this one was in the worst shape, but all of his Superbirds were 440 cars, which makes restoration and parts salvaging easier.

The tour was over and I was in shock from the collection's impressive content. And to this day I am in awe of the true generosity Mike showed me, someone he had just met, for sharing his collection with me. It goes to show there are still amazing people in the car hobby.

I'VE BEEN FORTUNATE TO BUILD a reputation as an honest journalist, and I have become part of a community on social media that allows me to tap into more people and finds than I could have imagined. In the 10 years or so I've been actively hunting for cool cars in barns, fields, and beyond, I thought I had found all the big-ticket items around Chicago. I was a member of the local clubs, went to area shows, and people knew what I did and how I do it. But sometimes things just come out of nowhere and surprise you. That's what happened when a gentleman named Tom messaged me through Facebook.

He had followed my work and asked if I knew of a pair of Aero Warriors—a 1969 Dodge Charger 500 and a 1970 Plymouth Superbird— sitting in a barn in Wisconsin. He said his friend Scott had these two cars in his barn, and that he'd be happy to show them to me. And they were only about two hours from my home. I jumped at the chance!

Pulling into Tom's, oh, let's call it a "compound," he gave me a tour of his shop and his projects. There was a Plymouth Duster, a Dodge Challenger, and a 1970 Plymouth GTX that had serious front-end damage under repair. Coolest of all, to me, was a really neat late-'70s Dodge Ramptruck Tom had purchased off of Craigslist.

With the grille safely inside the nearly empty passenger compartment, this original 1969 Dodge Charger 500 sits directly next to a few dozen hay bales and a 1970 Plymouth Superbird.

CHARGER BARN BURNER

We then headed to Scott's farm. I still couldn't believe I had never heard of this collection until a few days earlier.

Scott invited us up to the main barn, which, based on the old construction style, was at least 100 years old. And there, in the barn's center stall was what we were there for: a pair of legends.

There sat two of the rarest muscle cars in the world: a 1969 Dodge Charger 500 and a 1970 Superbird. It was clear the cars had not moved from the barn in a long time. There were marks from bird droppings on both vehicles, and with the barn actually used for hay storage, there was a good amount of hay tucked in the engine compartment of the 500. The Superbird had been spared most of the hay, but not the bird droppings.

Scott purchased the 1969 Dodge Charger after seeing it advertised in the local penny saver magazine. The owner said he thought it had been modified, and Scott knew immediately what he meant. Scott bought it and drove it for a short time, but the car was a bit beat, so he parked it with plans to restore it. Well, life happens and things get put on the back burner, so the car remained parked, mostly complete, for over 30 years.

Shortly after acquiring the 500, Scott saw an ad in an Aero Warrior club flyer for the Superbird in Iowa. Scott bought it, hauled it home, and unfortunately, it has been sidelined with the 500. He believed the engine wasn't built correctly and blew up, so previous owners had parted the car out. All Scott got was the main bodywork, engine, transmission, and rear end, but none of the original unique Superbird parts, such as the nose or rear wing. But he had since been able to acquire the missing parts.

Random parts were scattered about the barn: a six-barrel intake for the Superbird in a pile of hay, a spare grille for the 500 in an

OPPOSITE: A closeup of one quarter panel on the 1970 Superbird. Plymouth wanted people to know who produced such a unique car, and they successfully did it with large "PLYMOUTH" decals on each side of the Superbird on the quarter panels.

OPPOSITE BOTTOM: Another piece of the puzzle, a new old stock, never used Superbird nose. Scott found this nose shortly after he got the car. It has been in storage ever since. It's not the storage place I would use—with a spare desk and bikes— but whatever works!

INSET: You can get a better look at the rougher parts of the Charger 500, especially the quarter panels. But the really unique pieces, the aero rear window setup and trunk lid, are still with the car, as is the flush-mounted grille.

BELOW: The engine in the 1969 Charger 500 is a 440-cubic-inch V-8 that is mated to a four-speed manual transmission. It was driven home from Milwaukee and driven around for a short period of time before the owner put the car away to fix some issues.

ABOVE: Since the 1970 Superbird was missing many of the pieces that make the Superbird unique, like the wing and nose, the owner has been collecting pieces through the years to put the car back together. This is just a spare upright he has for the car. A complete wing is safely tucked away in the rafters.

LEFT: This is the view you get when walking into the barn for the first time: snowmobiles, a tower of hay, and a pair of rare Aero Warriors sitting in the middle. This is not something people think exists in the modern era, but there they are! And completely untouched.

actual barrel, and more. But the big-ticket items were in the basement of the farmhouse, including the NOS (new old stock) nose and the wing for the Superbird.

The term *barn find* is thrown around fairly liberally nowadays, but this was as legit as they come, and I was completely giddy with excitement.

We left the farm but stayed in touch with Scott, whose cars were included in the "Barn Finds and Hidden Gems" presentation I helped organize for the Muscle Car and Corvette Nationals in the fall of that year. Scott was so enthused by my excitement over his cars that he dug the 500 out of the barn and brought it straight to the show, its first show ever. This is what makes what I do absolutely worth it.

CHAPTER 2:
FORD & MER

FORD HAS ALWAYS BEEN A LEADER in automobiles since
Henry Ford perfected the assembly line and revolutionized the
entire car industry. Ford dropped another bomb on the world
when it introduced the Ford Mustang. While in some circles
Mustangs are considered pony cars, I've always considered
them muscle cars—even with one of the craziest engines
produced shoved between the fenders, the Boss 429. Ford has
a long history of offering cool cars with hot engines. In muscle
car discussions, Ford should not be known only for the Mustang,
but that's the model most people remember.

There were a few cars before the Mustang that could be
considered muscle cars. In 1963, there was the Falcon Sprint
and Mercury Comet S-22 that had the 260-cubic-inch V-8 out of
the larger Ford Fairlane. Just a year later, the Mustang debuted
on the Falcon platform, and with the Fairlane engine lineup. It
was a huge success, while the Falcon Sprint and Comet S-22
are footnotes to history.

Most people will say that the typical muscle car started
with the 1964 Pontiac GTO, and for a while at least, Ford really
didn't have anything in that same category. The Mustang was
still selling extremely well, better than the niche muscle cars.
Its market share was growing, and its base was young drivers
whom Ford wanted to nurture as brand-loyalist customers. Ford
had the Ford Galaxie, a full-size model in line with the Chevrolet
Impala and Dodge Monaco, but it wasn't a muscle car. It had

Not something you find much anymore, this 1966 Mustang Fastback was missing the entire floor. It
looked like someone had started a restoration, then just gave up. It sits rusting in the junkyard.

quite a history, though, as a cool car with a large selection of high-powered engines stuck between the front fenders. So Ford developed the midsized Fairlane and, at Mercury, the new-for-1966 Comet on the Fairlane platform as its muscle car fighters.

The Fairlane was in its fifth generation by 1966, and it looked the muscle car part: midsized and it could be equipped with just about every engine Ford had to offer, which Ford did. The Fairlanes and Comets had the GT, GTA, Cyclone, Cyclone GT, and Caliente models as their go-to muscle cars, and you could get them with every engine. Many were outfitted with the 390-cubic-inch V-8 that was standard in many of the models. It produced 335 base horsepower and had a four-barrel carburetor. If you understood the order sheet, though, you could order up something bigger: a 427!

It was not very well known you could get the 427 in the Fairlanes and Comets, but customers who ordered them had little rocket ships on their hands that could fight the Chevelle SS 454 and Hemi Road Runners on the street. The R-Code (as it was coded on the VIN) 427 was an engine with 425 brake horsepower, dual four-barrel carburetors, and Ford's "Top Loader" four-speed transmission as the only option for that engine.

In 1967, the Mustang got a facelift. It still was the same underneath, but it had a larger body. It carried over into 1968 basically unchanged, and in 1969 it received another body update

ABOVE: The Mustang was very well-optioned. Having rear window louvers on a 1969 Mach 1 is pretty rare, as is the shaker hood. But we were pretty sure the shaker was added on later.

TOP: Sitting for decades behind a house in rural Illinois, this poor 1969 Ford Mustang Mach 1 was owned by the property owner's son, who had left it there decades before.

What better way to stash a 1972 Mustang Sportroof in a junkyard, then putting it on top of another Mustang? Sadly, the lower 1969 Mustang Sportroof is the more desirable of the two.

INSET (LEFT TO RIGHT): By 1970, the Mustang had gotten a little bigger, and the fastback was now called the SportsRoof. This 1970 Mustang SportsRoof sits rusting in a Wisconsin junkyard, along with about 30 Tri-Five Chevrolets.

What was thought to be an original Shelby Mustang was actually a 1967 Mustang GT with a 390. This car was later campaigned by Manhattan Ford at numerous racetracks throughout the Northeast.

The 1967 Mustang was made to resemble a Shelby Mustang of the same years. It was purchased by the newest owner in 1971 at King Ford in Brooklyn, New York. He raced it on the street for a short time, then moved it out to his garage, where it has sat for about 30 years while the owner works on his other passion, racing.

that really made it look the part of a muscle car. And it had the different lineups to fight in every corner of the market. If you wanted a handling car, you could get the Boss 302 to compete with Camaro Z/28 or Challenger T/A. For all-out drag racing, the Mustang Boss 429 was a monster, and for everything in between there was the Mach 1.

Not to be outdone by the Mustang, Mercury developed its own muscle car, the Cougar. It was based on the same platform as the Fairlane and Mustang, but was intended to be the "upscale" muscle

OPPOSITE TOP: Owned by a gentleman in Detroit, this super low-mileage 1969 Mach 1 Mustang was loaded to the hilt with options, especially to go drag racing. It had sat in a garage in Detroit for a few decades. Now owned by the second owner, still in Detroit, it waits its turn to get freshened up and brought back to life.

OPPOSITE BOTTOM: A sad sight all the way around, these 1965 Mustang Fastbacks were in line for the crusher. They sat in a junkyard that had closed and was crushing out. The yard had opened the doors for a few months and allowed people to buy parts off of anything they could, while they could. So thankfully nothing of real value was lost.

FOLLOWING PAGES: This is something you will probably see nowhere else: twin green 1969 Mach 1 Mustangs stacked on top of each other. These were both very badly wrecked at some point, and sadly sit rusting away in a junkyard in Michigan.

BELOW: Another original Detroit Mustang, this time a 1967 Mustang GT Fastback in its original silver paint. It had been sitting for decades with a bad engine and transmission the new owner discovered.

car for the masses. A bit larger than the Mustang, its first generation ran from 1967 through 1970 with a wide variety of makes and models, some with the 427 and 428s. One of the most memorable was the introduction of the Cougar Eliminator in 1969 with wild colors and wilder equipment combinations, the rarest being two Cougar Eliminators produced for racing with Boss 429 engines.

The Fairlane and Comets got updates as well. In 1968, they went to a new, more Coke bottle shape in line with other muscle cars on the market. In addition to the redesign, there were different body styles within the same lineup. They now had a notchback, SportRoof (fastback), truck, and convertibles that had already been around for a few generations. The SportRoof did well and were able to carry almost the entire range of engines that Ford produced. The 427 was no longer available, however, while the 428-cubic-inch V-8 Cobra Jet engine was an new option.

In 1969, to compete with the success of the low-buck Plymouth Road Runner, Ford produced the Cobra on the Ford platform. It could use any of the engines, and with a wide variety of options. This was the same platform developed by Ford and Mercury for NASCAR that evolved into the Ford Talladega and Mercury Cyclone Spoiler.

As the muscle car era peaked, so did the offerings from Ford. The Mustang underwent a major design change in 1971, and in 1970, you had all the great engines available. The Fairlane and Comet were gone, replaced with the Torino and, for a short while, the Falcon.

The Cyclone still existed, but gone was the Cyclone CJ, as only the Spoiler and GT were available in 1970. These were available with just about every engine except the Boss 429, and they had their own unique engines, the 429 Cobra Jet and 429 Super Cobra Jet.

I would be remiss to not mention the Shelby Mustangs in muscle car history. They always had more horsepower then the regular Mustangs as well as better suspensions. It had been and always will be something special to have a Shelby, either from the early 1966 style to the more widely known 1967–1968 style with the big air scoops and other Shelby equipment, or the more commonly forgotten 1969 and 1970 Shelby Mustangs. Sadly, unsold 1969 Shelby Mustangs were given new VINs legally as 1970 models. Still to this day, if you have a Shelby Mustang, it doesn't get much better than that!

Things started winding down after 1971 and the Mustang was redesigned again, this time looking longer. Most people are not fond of the 1971–1973 model years even though this span included one of the best all-around muscle cars ever, the 1971 Boss

BELOW AND INSET: This is not just a regular Mercury Cougar, this is a full-blown 1970 Cougar Eliminator, just about the top of the tree when it comes to Cougars. This one even has the large 428 Cobra Jet and a 4-speed transmission. It has been sitting in the yard next to the tobacco barn and corn field for decades on end. It isn't in terrible shape, though.

TOP: This poor Cougar has had a rough life and is now wasting away in a Michigan junkyard. Sadly, someone stuck Mustang GT badges on it.

INSET (LEFT TO RIGHT): The back half of a Cougar sticks out of the weeds. Hopefully, the front half went to save another car or two.

Saved from the scrapper, this Cougar now resides in a cow pasture until the owner is able to find a home for it.

351 Mustang. The Torino and Cyclone were basically unchanged into 1971, and by 1972 that all changed, as the Torino had a redesign and the Cyclone was an option on the Mercury Montego. Unfortunately, after 1971 the government and insurance companies came down hard on muscle cars. Pollution controls on engines and sky-high insurance rates for muscle cars basically killed them off.

They didn't die completely, though. The Torino would go on a few more years, getting fame with the TV series *Starsky & Hutch*. But the one that made it through everything was the Mustang. It adapted with the times and eventually led the resurgence in performance with the Fox Body Mustang platform starting in 1979. That platform lasted in some form until 2004 and helped kick off the modern muscle car wars, where Ford had a front-line seat with its imposing new Mustangs.

WHILE HEADING TO THE WELLBORN
MUSEUM to assist in the 2015 Aero Warriors
Reunion, I had a few free days to explore the
area. I got a few leads from people online, and
a guy name Eddie informed me that he had a
field full of cars! That piqued my interest, and we
planned to meet.

As I pulled up to Eddie's place, he released
his three "vicious attack" dachshunds, each of
whom jumped off the porch, ran directly to my
car, and within seconds claimed a tire and were
relieving themselves on it. Eddie and I laughed,
then headed to the metal storage barn where
some of the nicer cars were stashed.

The building was filled with cool Fords.
Immediately in front of us was an extremely rare,
first-generation Ford Lightning that toured the
country with the auto shows. Along the wall
was a 1970 Mach 1 Mustang, and there was
also a pair of blue Mustangs: a new 2008 Shelby
Mustang and a 1968 Mustang Fastback. A 1992
GMC Syclone sport truck was tucked away in
the corner, and probably the coolest car in the
building was a 1970 Ford Torino. It was an export
car with several options that weren't available in
the United States, including electric rear window
defrost and kilometer dashboard. You wouldn't
expect to find it sitting in a barn in Alabama!

This cherry 1969 Mach 1 Mustang drew my eye as we entered the garage.
Black car with red stripes. Kind of an odd combination that it came
with the 390-cubic-inch V-8. Very few were made with that option. This
one only really needed to be cleaned up and gone through to be a real
thoroughbred again.

OPPOSITE: Driving to a friend's house in Alabama, I encountered something bizarre—a wall-less Alabama barn full of Ford muscle cars, including a bevy of Mustangs.

OPPOSITE INSET (LEFT TO RIGHT): Just about my favorite Ford out there, this 1970 Mach 1 Mustang with shaker in blue is right up there. This has been sitting, buried in this storage building for many years. But what a better way to keep it safe than building a wall between the car and everything else?!

A 1968 Mustang coupe sits in the corner of a dirt floor storage building. This is a nice, nearly complete car that is in really nice shape. It is just dirty from sitting in storage for so long.

OPPOSITE BOTTOM: In their friend's garage was a few neat pieces of Ford muscle. This is a bigger offering that Ford had in 1970, a Ford Torino Cobra. In bright orange even. This had been sitting for a while neglected, but the owner is a serious Ford guy, so the car, even while sitting, is protected from the elements. This one was equipped with the big Ford engine, the 429.

BELOW: This was the complete opposite of the rest. This is another 1969 Mach 1 Mustang, this one had a very hard life. This was rescued from a guy who was going to crush all the cars in his yard, and the owner and his friends couldn't see that happen. So here the car sits, in better shape than what it was heading for.

Another small storage shed housed a 1966 Mustang notchback and a really nice first-generation Bronco that matched the 1968 and 2008 Mustangs in the first barn. Elsewhere on the property were a 1969 Chevelle, a 1956 Ford two-door, and a few Jeeps. In the main shop, where bodywork and general maintenance were handled, were some nice Ford Mavericks and a 1955 Chevrolet Bel Air. Along one wall was a 1970 Mustang SportsRoof that I was told was one of two produced for a Ford executive. Yet Eddie said the VIN was one off from a car that had gone through an auction on TV and was nearly identical, so you never know.

In the fields behind the shop were several first-generation Mustangs, most of them notchbacks. There was also a smattering of Mavericks of many model years, and an oddball such as a rear-ended 1969 Road Runner and a Chevelle.

At Eddie's dad's place, just across the road, were more buildings full of cars, as well as a few dozen outside or in lean-tos. A grouping of 1955–1957 Chevrolets were out back, keeping the company of Ford Fairlanes and Mercury Comets, first-gen Mustangs, and a few Yugos! In a lean-to were my favorite vehicles: a nice, mostly original 1966 Mustang Fastback and a 1970 Ford Torino station wagon that was so untouched, when you opened the doors, it still smelled like a new car. That's how low-mileage and mint the car was.

Inside the storage barn was another first-generation Ford Lighting, one that had been in an accident and was totaled before it was even sold; it was parted out and Eddie bought it and put it away with single-digit mileage. He has another worn-out Lighting he intends to part out to fix the low-mileage one. Other vehicles on site include a 1967 Mustang Notchback, a 1970 four-door Plymouth Belvedere, and a 1970 AMC Javelin.

We headed to Eddie's friend Randy's place, and it turned out Randy's shop was a Ford lover's dream. There were Ford engine treasures everywhere, such as a smattering of SOHC engine parts,

Tunnel Ram small-block and big-block Ford pieces. Mounted to the wall was something I had never heard of before: the top of a "Cross Boss" intake manifold, a very rare intake sold over the counter at Ford dealerships mainly for Boss Mustangs.

In an attached garage was a surprising quartet of Ford products, including a very nice daily driver 1967 Mustang Fastback. There was also a sinister, black-and-red 1969 Mustang Mach 1, a very rare 390-cubic-inch V-8 car; a 1970 Ford Torino Cobra that was dirty from sitting for such a long period of time; and a 1970 Mustang convertible.

I thought we had seen everything, but we headed across the cow pasture in an off-road vehicle to access rows of muscle cars of all varieties. A junkyard owner was going to crush them all, but Eddie and his friends bought them all and put them in the pasture while they thought about what to do with them. The cows sure didn't mind!

The field revealed everything from a 1964 Chevrolet Impala SS to a 1972 Dodge Challenger Rallye, and a variety of Ford products, including a few Ford Torinos, Rancheros, and even another 1969 Mustang Mach 1 or two. There were at least 25 to 30 cars in the field when I visited, and to my knowledge, they all have since been sold. It's hard to forget talking in the field near a 1966 Plymouth Fury when along came a huge cow to the other side of the car. It was one of those moments I'll never forget. A 1969 Mustang Sportsroof, 1970 Mustang convertible, 1971 Torino convertible, 1963 Falcon Sprint, and 1967 Mustang Fastback sat in some other buildings on the property as well.

Out in the open barn was another collection of Ford Torinos of the late '60s and early '70s style that are so popular, a 1970 Mustang Grande, and even an early 1960s Ford Fairlane. It was incredible to see such a collection of cars just sitting out, mostly in the open, with very little rust on them. If anything, they had a green algae, moss, or mold on many surfaces, but thankfully there's not much harm in that. The dry summers, mild winters, and no salt on the roads keep them pretty safe.

It was an absolutely mind-blowing experience seeing these collections of Fords. My world usually centers around Mopars, but to come across such a good group of guys with such cool collections of Fords, it gives me hope I'll get to see more like this in the future.

ABOVE: In all my travels, I don't see very many 1971 Ford Ranchero GTs to say the least. And this one was in bright green. Another rescued car, this one was actually in pretty decent shape for sitting for so long.

RIGHT: This 1971 Ford Torino has not been sitting that much, just enough to get a light coating of dust on the car. What makes this rare is the car was built for export. Had a bunch of unique export only options, such as electric window defroster, kilometer speedometer, and unique power window setup.

AK EPP 6005

TOP: Rescued from the yard along with the rest, this 1967 Mustang Fastback was quite the hot rod in its day, with yellow paint job and pink stripes. Not my cup of tea, but it was for someone. This was tucked all the way in the back of the farm field, far from the cows.

MIDDLE: In the last stall in the garage we were shown this clean 1970 Mustang Convertible. It currently had a 351 between the fender wells. It did not need a lot of work to get out on the road, just as many people know, things get in the way and put on the back burner.

BOTTOM: Model year 1970 was the last year of this Mustang in the SportsRoof style. This one without side scoops could have been a Boss Mustang, but nothing showed it as being one. Just a cool Mustang that a yard owner got at some point and was going to crush before the current owners saved it.

OPPOSITE TOP: The midsize at the time 1971 Ford Torino Convertible. This one is another car put away for a rainy day in the peanut factory. Was not in bad shape, it has just been sitting for a while. It has the famous laser stripe down the side.

OPPOSITE INSET (LEFT TO RIGHT): Not something you see very often, a 1969 Fairlane Fastback, the same car that was changed into the Talladegas for NASCAR. This one isn't a race version or even a GT, but is a standard version sitting in the open barn.

This poor Torino has seen better days, and while it does look rough, it isn't really that rusty, even when sitting in an open barn. The shaker hood means it was something special like the GT or Cobra.

OPPOSITE BOTTOM: A very rare offering from Ford, the 1963 Ford Falcon Futura. This was a great combo with the 260-cubic-inch V-8 with a black exterior and red interior. This is *was*—a running and driving car and was just stuck in the factory while the owner works on other projects. It needed a going-through and wash to make it a great car.

TOP: A 1970 Torino quietly waits its turn in the barn. With a few projects ahead of it, this bare-bones Torino might be sitting a little while.

MIDDLE: Another unique Ford muscle product, a 1966 Fairlane. These are few and far between, as they were not as popular as other midsized offerings such as the Chevelle or Charger. This was someone's hot rod, with yellow and black paint on what remained of the body.

BOTTOM: Can't miss the bright blue on this 1971 Torino. This blue stands out among all the other Ford products under the barn.

ABOVE: This 1966 Mustang Fastback sat partially outside of a lean-to for many years, and in the Alabama environment the mold and mildew ran rampant on the bright orange paint. Thankfully the body was solid, however, and only really needed a good wash to return it to a presentable state.

A FRIEND EMAILED ME, asking if I knew anything about a Mustang he had found online. I checked the link and learned this was not an ordinary Ford Mustang, but it was an extremely rare 1966 Ford Shelby Mustang GT350H, with the H standing for Hertz Rent-a-Car.

In 1966, Hertz Rent-a-Car and Shelby collaborated on a unique vehicle and rental package. Shelby produced a 1966 Shelby GT350H exclusively for Hertz that had the upgraded 289-cubic-inch V-8 of the regular Mustang, stiffer suspension, race tachometer, unique stripes just above the rocker panels, and more. This was no slouch, and it was just what Hertz wanted.

Hertz had this car for its Sports Car Club. You could rent this car from your local Hertz agency, go racing all weekend, and then return it Sunday night. Some people took these rent-a-racers, pulled the special parts, and swapped in regular Mustang parts, so many of these cars today don't have their original drivelines.

I arranged to meet with the car's owner, a widow who had owned it with her late husband and had decided to sell the car. As I pulled in the driveway, the Shelby sat just off to the side of the driveway underneath a car cover. The car was originally from California and was rented at a Hertz location in Los Angeles—but not for long,

You can see by the back third that the car is definitely well patina'd from years of being outdoors. It even looks as though the original spare tire is on the passenger side rear! You can't mistake that black and gold stripes though.

IT HERTZ

as Judy and her husband bought the car in St. Louis in 1967, a year before they got married. They drove the car everywhere, including on family vacations and adventures all over the country. They rolled up over 100,000 miles on it over the years.

Unfortunately, time took its toll on the car, and Judy's husband put it away with hopes they would restore it later in life and enjoy it once again. That time did not come, and her husband passed away in January 2015. It was his forethought that saved the car, though. As rare as these Shelby models were, many, especially the rental car variety, were beaten and abused and tossed away. But not this car. Judy's husband had been a pack rat and had saved everything from the car.

Sadly, the car had endured many years of Chicago weather, but the vehicle beneath the tattered old cover was treasure for sure: a real, complete 1966 Shelby GT350H Mustang. The most recent tabs on the license plate were from 1982. I had only seen restored examples of the car, never one in such condition. While it was complete, it wasn't perfect. Everything was there, but the elements had taken their toll. The bumpers were rusting, every panel had rust or rot, and the passenger-side quarter panel looked as though something heavy had fallen on it, crushing it a few inches.

I noticed the missing bottoms of the quarters, the holes in the rockers, and dents in the roof and body panels. Surprisingly, the rear

ABOVE: This gives you a better idea of what the car had been through, with a snow tire on the driver side rear. This car was a daily driver after being bought from Hertz as a used car. The husband and wife would travel all around the country in this car.

TOP: This shot was taken while standing atop a retaining wall, looking down at the poor 1966 Shelby GT350H. The "H" stands for Hertz Rent-a-Car. It doesn't really look that bad from this angle. You can see it is a little rusty, a bit crusty, but it is all there for someone to build upon.

INSET TOP: Still safely mounted to the dash of the Shelby, the tach was unique to the Shelby's at the time with custom emblem. This tach went all the way up to 9,000 rpm, but someone set the orange needle at just under 6,500 rpm to be safe.

INSET BOTTOM: It sure did look like the original 289 under the hood. I couldn't tell because of the dirt and leaves. But it had all the correct parts to be the original 289 that the car was born with. Usually people would rent the car, take the engine out, and swap in a regular 289. This looks to be the exception.

BOTTOM RIGHT: Looking over the interior, it is complete from front to back, but well worn. The original Shelby Steering Wheel and Tachometer are still attached where they should be.

wheel and tire on the passenger side looked like they were original. We guessed there was the full-size spare tire and that at some point, it had been put on—and left on. On the other side was a regular steel wheel with a snow tire.

Under the hood, things were much better. It looked like it had the right engine, and the correct pieces were all there, but I didn't have the ability to check numbers at the time. It had sat for some time without an air cleaner assembly, so the engine no doubt would need a rebuild. Other than an aftermarket alarm system, and various wear parts, the car looked mostly stock, and even had the original Shelby VIN tag affixed to the driver's-side inner fender.

Inside the car, the seats looked good, and the dash was intact and had the correct gauges. The extremely rare woodgrain Shelby steering wheel was there, and the Shelby tachometer was still affixed to the dashboard. A closer look revealed the downside, such as the door rusting away on both sides and the floors you could see through. At one point I noticed how sunny it was inside the car, but it wasn't sunny inside the car. The floor was gone and I was seeing the sun beneath it!

The car was an incredible time capsule. Judy told me some time later that someone had purchased the car and it was going to be fully restored on the West Coast. You never know what might happen with these cars that sit so long!

SOMEONE HAD GIVEN ME THE TIP that there was a junkyard in the Michigan woods still full of vintage cars. Sadly, yards like this don't exist much anymore. I know of a handful that in recent years have crushed everything, and many of the Michigan yards had gone away, so I was pleasantly surprised by what I found.

While in Detroit, I had some time and took a drive to see what I could find. Dejected by my early stops, I headed to the last one I could reach before it started getting dark, and it ended up being the mother lode of the month.

As soon as I saw vintage vehicles scattered near the main gate, I knew I was in the right spot. This was going to be good. After hearing what I do, a gentleman offered to show me around personally. He asked if the new Challenger I was driving was fast, and said that nothing was as quick as his old Fox Body Mustang. Oh boy, I thought!

The place had everything I could have hoped for in a junkyard. There were old motorcycles, snowmobiles, and all sorts of hot rods and muscle cars. There was a 1967 Mustang Fastback GT with its rear end sitting in the pond—a real 390-cubic-inch V-8 car. The Mustang was complete, but in bad shape. When I lifted the hood, the hood hinges stayed in place. They had completely rusted off of the hood, it was that bad.

I walked right past this car the first time because it is so buried. But a real 1967 Mustang GT Fastback—390 car that is sitting on the edge of a pond. And that's only when I saw it, the water level gets any higher and it would be IN the pond.

CHAPTER 2

I saw one of my favorite cars overall, a 1969 Mustang Mach 1. The car on its own is cool, but this blue Mach 1 was perched atop an old school bus! The engine was gone, as was most of the running gear, but it was a real Mach 1. After climbing on top of a conveniently parked tow truck, I could see the car more clearly, and it was bad. I thought having it on top of the bus would protect it and let it survive, but that was not the case. There was no glass in the vehicle, so everything had rotted—frame rails, body supports, you name it. I could see right through the frame.

Nearby was a neat oddity: a 1972 Dodge Travco motor home. An old motor home in a junkyard isn't odd, but this was the original, Class A-style motor home, and Travco units were built an hour or so from where the yard was located. They aren't common today, so finding one was interesting, to say the least.

There were numerous General Motors products in the yard, including quite a few GTOs and Chevelle SS models (which you'll see elsewhere in this book). We next came across another 1969 Mustang Mach 1, this one in even worse shape than the first, and it didn't have the luxury of being stored off the ground. It was badly rusted, but at least it still had parts of its interior and an engine, transmission, and rear axle assembly. It sat next to a 1970 Chevrolet Malibu that at some point been fitted with a factory 1970 Chevelle SS cowl induction hood!

The yard's owner knew the history of every car. He told me about how he had driven this car to go racing, or that car for adventuring.

BELOW: This is a 1969 Mach 1 Mustang, sitting on top of a *bus*. Not only is it sitting on top of a bus, but the door has been hanging open so long, a tree has grown up in the gap between. This was a bare-bones 351-cubic-inch V-8 2v car. But it was one of the first things you see walking in this yard.

ABOVE: This once-great 1967 Mustang Fastback has seen better days. The hood (unseen) had rotted completely off the hinges, but the aging beauty was complete

RIGHT: Just another 1969 Mach 1 Mustang lounging around in the yard in Michigan. This was another basic 351 cubic-inch V-8 car. This time not sitting on top of a bus, but that didn't help. The windows had been open for who knows how long and the engine was long gone. Still cool to see in a salvage yard though.

SOMEONE HAD GIVEN ME THE TIP that there was a junkyard in the Michigan woods still full of vintage cars. Sadly, yards like this don't exist much anymore. I know of a handful that in recent years have crushed everything, and many of the Michigan yards had gone away, so I was pleasantly surprised by what I found.

While in Detroit, I had some time and took a drive to see what I could find. Dejected by my early stops, I headed to the last one I could reach before it started getting dark, and it ended up being the mother lode of the month.

As soon as I saw vintage vehicles scattered near the main gate, I knew I was in the right spot. This was going to be good. After hearing what I do, a gentleman offered to show me around personally. He asked if the new Challenger I was driving was fast, and said that nothing was as quick as his old Fox Body Mustang. Oh boy, I thought!

The place had everything I could have hoped for in a junkyard. There were old motorcycles, snowmobiles, and all sorts of hot rods and muscle cars. There was a 1967 Mustang Fastback GT with its rear end sitting in the pond—a real 390-cubic-inch V-8 car. The Mustang was complete, but in bad shape. When I lifted the hood, the hood hinges stayed in—place. They had completely rusted off of the hood, it was that bad.

OPPOSITE TOP: The yard had a few other Mercury products in it, but this 1969 Cougar was just about the best one around. It actually didn't look that bad from the outside, but when you look inside you could see that the car had almost nothing underneath, including no floor boards.

OPPOSITE MIDDLE: Now this is something you don't see very often, two 1966 Mustang Fastbacks sitting next to each other in a junkyard. And both of them were really rough, but not beyond help. But the fact that the yard had two and placed them together just makes for a really interesting scene.

OPPOSITE BOTTOM: A bit further into the yard sits this 1972 Torino GT with rear window louvers. It's rare to find a Torino GT at all, but one with window louvers is crazy. They might not have come from this car; you never know in a salvage yard.

BELOW: Something a little bit different, this time a 1970 Mustang Mach 1. Another one with the smaller engine. But this one had nothing as it sat, rusting in the yard. This one had been beat up pretty good and was rusty throughout.

I WAS IN FOR ANOTHER SURPRISE not far from where I live after I saw a car junkie named Lance posting some cool finds on his Instagram account, and I inquired about them. He said they were his family's collection and I was welcome to see it with his dad.

Eventually, Lance and I met up at the Fall Jefferson Car Show & Swap Meet in Jefferson, Wisconsin, and I arranged to see the dad's collection. I had no idea he was less than an hour drive from where I lived in Wisconsin, but fall is a very busy time for me, so it took time to connect.

Lance, his father, and some friends were trying to consolidate some of his vehicles in a barn they had. It wasn't one of those steel buildings, or a new-age barn. It was a true, old wooden barn in Wisconsin. When Lance and his dad bought the barn, they cut out every other support beam so they could fit more cars inside.

Who would need so much room, you ask? Well, a family of gearheads, that's who. On Sundays after church, Lance's father and his father would buy a Penny Saver at the local gas station, then go pick up a $50 car. They preferred cars from Ford and its divisions, but not exclusively, so for years they went around the state, picking up cars and dragging them home.

Not something you see very often, not only is this a Mercury Cyclone Spoiler GT, but a convertible as well. While being stashed in a barn for a few decades didn't do great things for it, it didn't make the car any worse. This is one of a handful painted Indy Red, like the Comet GT Convertible Indy Pace Car of that year.

CYCLONES

LEFT: Relegated to the back corner of the barn, this poor 1964 Mustang convertible is in pretty rough shape, with rust throughout the body. Thankfully so much of Mustang sheet metal is reproduced, this car can come back from this without much issue. This one sported the rare 260-cubic-inch V-8, which was dropped quickly from the Mustang lineup, in favor of the 289.

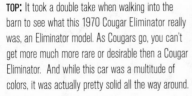

TOP: It took a double take when walking into the barn to see what this 1970 Cougar Eliminator really was, an Eliminator model. As Cougars go, you can't get more much more rare or desirable then a Cougar Eliminator. And while this car was a multitude of colors, it was actually pretty solid all the way around.

TOP RIGHT: Just sitting outside a large storage barn is a 1965 Falcon Futura convertible. This was the sportier version of the Falcon. Unfortunately the years sitting outside have destroyed the top and rusted out much of the understructure. Thankfully it shares much with the Mustang so it is not beyond saving.

(I grew up in the wrong era!) Eventually, their passion grew into the Wisconsin Dells Auto Museum.

The museum showcased a wide variety of cars that they owned, and they had plenty to rotate through the small location. They really loved factory pace cars, the cars that ran ahead of race cars at major races such as the Indianapolis 500. Unfortunately, a fire in one of the storage buildings damaged about 55 cars, some beyond help. In 2005, with the father's business keeping him busy, they closed the museum for good.

This was epic, with not just one or two cars, but barns—barns!—full of cars. It blew me away. As I pulled up, I came upon a 1965 Ford Falcon Futura convertible, white with a red interior—it was sure a looker. I said I was sad to see this neat car outside, and Lance said not to worry, there was a nice one in the other building!

The first barn was full of cars from wall to wall. I hadn't seen anything like that in a long time. There was a Studebaker pace car that had been damaged in the fire and was nothing but a husk, although you could just make out the lettering on the doors. Behind that was a 1963 Chevrolet Impala SS convertible with its 409 W-head V-8 engine sitting in the dirt directly in front of the car! (You'll see that elsewhere in the book.)

And then there was a car that is one of my personal favorites, a Mercury Comet. This wasn't just any Mercury Comet, but a Comet Cyclone GT convertible, the same model used as the official pace car of the 1966 Indianapolis 500. This was one of the factory cars prepped like the one used at the track. This one wasn't quite as nice as some of the others, but after being relegated to a barn, likely for decades, it was in good shape.

Just beyond a wall was something kind of odd, a very early 1964 Mustang convertible. What made it odd was it had a 260-cubic-inch V-8, which was available for only a short time before Ford started dropping the 289-cubic-inch V-8 into the Mustang. And it was a convertible, making it even rarer.

Directly across the barn from the Mustang was a really cool piece of history, a 1970 Mercury Cougar Eliminator with the very desirable 302-cubic-inch V-8 that is more commonly associated with its Mustang brethren, the Boss 302 Mustang. While it looked rough, this was Lance's car, and he has his entire life ahead of him to put the car together. Or drive it as is! You never know.

The building also held several GM and Ford big-body cars from the '70s, a limo, a convertible, and a few more cool muscle cars, including a 1971 Ford Torino GT convertible. That was cool in its own right, but it also had the shaker hood option, which elevated the coolness factor. I cannot imagine cruising down the street with the top down and the shaker shaking as you drove. The car was rusty, but not beyond help, and with the cool combo of color and options, it should be saved.

There was also another Indy Pace Car, a 1966 Mercury Comet Cyclone GT convertible. This one was in a bit worse shape than the first, but not terrible, and it looked complete other than missing a few odds and ends. Nearby was another convertible, this one a 1965 Ford

BELOW INSET: Another, less complete, 1966 Comet Cyclone GT convertible. This one has not had as good a life as the one further forward in the barn. But even with it being in a bit rougher shape, it still is a very rare car with it being another one painted like the Indy Pace Car Cyclone of that year.

BOTTOM: Standing out in the barn is hard in this group of cars, but a bright blue 1971 Torino GT convertible with a shaker hood sure does check all the boxes in my book. Definitely rotted pretty well though, it was rescued and safely stashed away in the barn, until the time it can be worked on.

TOP: In another barn was a few more Ford products, including this little worse for wear 1970 Torino Cobra with shaker hood. This one definitely needed a good amount of work to be nice. It had been sitting for a long time, and now finally is safely in a nice and dry garage.

INSET ABOVE: Tucked all the way in the very back corner of the barn, this 1965 Ford Galaxie 500 convertible was basically stock. Still having the original hubcaps and everything. These were the cars that you wanted to cruise around in. And this one looked as though a good wash and some new tires and you could probably do just that.

Galaxie 500, and there was another Mustang convertible, this one with the newer 289-cubic-inch V-8 under the hood.

More cars, most of them very nice, were packed in another storage building, including a 1968 Shelby GT500KR convertible and a 1970 Ford Torino Cobra with the shaker hood. This latter car was cool, with a black-out hood, shaker hood scoop, red paint, and a black interior. It was likely quite the looker when new, but now had rust everywhere; it could be saved, and probably will, but will require a lot of cash. Close by was another 1966 Mercury Comet Cyclone GT convertible, this one light blue and not a pace car. Even when buried among all these cars, it looked good!

To top off the day, the father took us to a garage of his that had a few beautifully restored cars. But buried in the corner—and I do mean buried—was another 1968 Shelby GT500KR convertible. He had blasted it apart to fix it, but life gets busy and the car got put on the back burner, especially since he had another one that runs. So this one sits, waiting to be put back together, with everything right there: engine, transmission, NOS (new old stock) trim, original wheels—everything!

With the sun setting, I headed home. It took me a while to digest everything I had seen in just a few short hours. It was so kind of them to take their time and let me ogle their collection. But I also believe they enjoyed seeing me get so excited about the cars, so everyone wins in the end!

ON ONE OF THE WEB PAGES I FOLLOW, a guy named Matt posted photos of a cool car in his barn, a 1967 Mercury Comet. What really blew me away was it was a very rare Comet, so I commented on his post; we quickly learned that he lived less than an hour from my house, so away I went!

As I pulled onto his farmstead, I immediately saw the tail end of the Comet in the barn! I was surprised that the car had sat here for decades, and I had literally passed this area numerous times on my travels, and I somehow missed it every time.

It was an old barn, with river stones as the foundation, and large, hand-cut wooden beams and slats. It was a classic old red barn. The lower level had been used to house animals (and there were still a few chickens and cats running around), but you could also see the remains of decades of farm use.

And there, in the doorway, was a different sort of animal: an R-Code 1967 Mercury Comet. Most people didn't know that there was a Mercury Comet in 1967, including me, before I saw this one. But they were produced right along with the Cougar. The 1967 options let you equip them in a variety of ways, from the bare-bones 202 model with a post and inline six, to the top of the top: the R-Code that included

With the restoration of the 1967 Fairlane not needing a bunch, but still needing some parts, this parts car was acquired to fulfill the need when it arises. Still not much was needed, so while it is in rough shape, it probably isn't beyond help for someone.

STOCK

32   33

32   33

TOP: I did not know that such a vehicle existed until my friend showed me this one. I thought that the Comet brand ended around 1965. But since it was basically an upscale version of the Ford Falcon, it continued right along with it. This 427 Comet came with the dual scoop hood normally seen on the Cyclone model.

INSET (LEFT TO RIGHT): This poor old 1963 Ford Galaxie was not as lucky, sitting in the dirt in the side yard in Wisconsin. This poor car probably will live again, but it would need a bit of work.

The rear end of this 1967 Comet has been open to the elements for years, with no barn door existing anymore to keep the weather out. But even with it sitting like it is, the car is extremely solid, and just has great patina now. The chickens don't help though.

the 427-cubic-inch V-8 with two four-barrel carburetors. Not many people got the R-Code Comet when they could get a Mustang or Cougar, each of which was a much sportier option. Even the Comet lineup had a sporty option, the Cyclone. The car I was viewing wasn't any of those. It was rarer then all of them.

This car had been special ordered by Dick Garbo of Garbo Motors in Racine, Wisconsin, for use in racing. But it had a weird set of options. It had the big 427 with the two four-barrels, and a four-speed to go through the gears. But most R-Code Comets were built as stripped-down 202 models—the lighter, the better.

Out back on the property in Wisconsin, this 1963 Ford Fairlane 500 sits in pretty good shape for sitting. This one coming with the fairly desirable 260 cubic-inch V-8. It looks rough with all the assortment of parts and junk on it, but it really wasn't too bad for sitting.

This one went the opposite direction. It was optioned with the Caliente body, which got the courtesy light group, a rear-seat speaker, tinted glass, disc brakes, a black vinyl top and black interior, and onyx black paint.

Dick raced the car like that for some time, then sold it. It eventually made its way into the hands of Matt's father-in-law, a die-hard Ford/Mercury guy. He raced it for a few years, and then the car was put away, with the engine and transmission pulled for proper storage. The license plate on the car had a 1981 tab.

They submitted the car's information to Marti Auto Works for a Marti Report on the car. Marti Auto Works has access to Ford's info database and can tell you the makeup and rarity of your car. The report on this car said this was one of only two R-Code Comets built in this configuration.

This wasn't the only rare car the father-in-law owned. He came over while we were inspecting the Comet and invited us to see what he had at his farm nearby. I didn't know what to expect, and when we arrived, I saw the farm was littered with Ford and Mercury products of all shapes and sizes. Our first stop was his main workshop, which was filled with all sorts of high-performance goodness, such as several 427 engines, spare parts and pieces, even the valve cover to

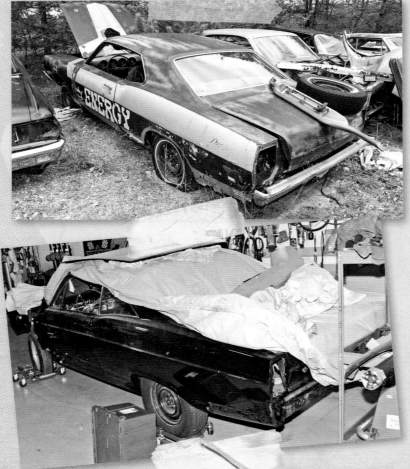

TOP: One of the coolest cars out on the property in Wisconsin was this Ford Galaxie, that was used as a drag car. The original painted on lettering is still visible on the car. Sadly, the car is nothing but a shell, but the patina of the car is unmatched. You can't buy that look, no matter how hard you try.

MIDDLE: One of my personal favorites was this 1969 Ford Fairlane. It had a 1970's paint job on it with branding and such. But wasn't very "race car-ish." It was definitely someone's hot rod at some point. Might have even been a Cobra Fairlane, but the Cobra painted on the passenger side of the trunk lid. Right next to the saying, "Going through the motions."

BOTTOM: Not to be outdone, the father-in-law, who lives nearby, has a collection of cool Ford and Mercury products hanging around. This is another rare one, a 1967 Ford Fairlane R-Code car. So it has the same 427 cubic-inch V-8 with dual four barrel carburetors. The production number shows that this car and the Comet were not far off from each other on the production line back in 1967.

a rare SOHC (single overhead cam) Ford 427 engine hanging on the wall. If you were a Ford guy, this shop was your happy place.

There was a really neat 1967 Ford Fairlane R-Code with the same engine combination as the Comet we saw earlier. The production numbers on both cars were pretty close, meaning they were probably built on the same line at roughly the same time. This Fairlane was in the midst of a restoration even though it only had 277 miles on the odometer.

The shop held a few other cool vehicles such as a nice '60s Ford Galaxie, a low-mile 1993 Mustang Cobra, and a sharp 1966 Mercury Marauder. Outside were the vehicles with more patina, and they were more in my wheelhouse, such as the variety of Ford Galaxies and Fairlanes. Some were old race cars, parts cars, or future projects. These vehicles might not be as desirable as other cars, but finding parts is hard, so you get every parts car you can, just to make one or two good ones.

The yard also held more project and parts cars, including a 1967 Mercury Comet 202 that had endured a hard life and was rotted in half. But it had everything the R-Code car might need, so it was still of value. The coolest car was the old circle-track Ford Torino that was still in its "as raced" condition. It had been parted out over the years, but the original signage was still there, including hand-painted lettering and vintage stickers. Most cars like this had been sent to

In my many travels, I cannot remember seeing a 1964 Mercury Marauder. The "hot rod" of the larger Mercury lineup. These things usually had the biggest engine and heavy-duty suspension and transmission. The one is missing a few parts for another Marauder sadly.

ABOVE: Just about the complete opposite of the 427 Comet in the barn, this is a parts car for that one. This is a 1967 Comet 202, the base model. It still looks good, but if you look closer, you can see that the nose of the vehicle is at a different angle than the main body of the car sadly.

LEFT: Another 1964 Marurader stashed away at the farm in Wisconsin. This one in worse shape than the previous one, but still a hard to find vehicle. The owner collected them through the years, knowing how hard parts were to attain, for when the time came to restore the few that he has.

the crusher, but this one was "saved" and would end its days in a Ford guy's front yard.

I had an absolute blast hanging out with Matt and his family, seeing not only the Comet, but his father-in-law's collection as well. It blew my mind that all this was here, but you would never have known if you didn't know the family. And I'm lucky enough now to consider them my friends.

TOP: Another high-performance offering at the farm in Wisconsin, this time a 1962 Ford Galaxie 500 with the big 390 cubic-inch V-8 under the hood, or at least it did. This one looked too high in the nose still have that large powerplant under the hood. But even for sitting, the car looked to be extremely clean.

MIIDDLE: An outlier in the group was this 1964 Galaxie 500XL, as there were no other vehicles like this around. But since the owner saw a derelict Ford product, he couldn't let that be, so he dragged it home and left it in the field for a time when he might use it or part with it sadly.

BOTTOM RIGHT: This poor Ford Torino Fastback had a hard life of racing. Heavily modified for probably circle-track work. There isn't much left to the old car now after so many years. The original painted-on advertising and decals are neat to see, since most cars of the period are either restored or destroyed!

IF YOU GO BY THE NORMAL IDENTIFICATION of a muscle car—a big engine in a smaller body—it all started with General Motors (GM). I don't mean the GTO either. It started way back in 1949! Oldsmobile rolled out the Rocket 88. It was the smaller body, but had the bigger high-compression V-8. There were others since then that toyed with that same idea. Chrysler had the 300 with the Hemi lineups. Ford had its share with the Thunderbolts and such. But most people say the proper use of term started with the 1964 Pontiac GTO.

It started with the idea of dropping the big 389-cubic-inch V-8 engine from Pontiac's full-size Catalina in the engine compartment of the midsized Tempest. At the time, the largest engine you could get in the Tempest was the 326-cubic-inch V-8. There was a sportier option already available, the Le Mans, but it still retained the original 326. Wanting to sell the street performance, Pontiac called its car the GTO, which stood for Gran Turismo Omologato, and was inspired by Ferrari race cars at the time. In some circles, it was called the "Grand Tempest Option."

That really kicked things off, especially at GM. Almost overnight there were high-performance versions of all of each GM brand's cars built on the A-body platform, such as the Tempest. Chevrolet had the Chevelle Malibu, while Oldsmobile had the 442 (4-barrel carburetor, 4-speed, dual exhaust, originally), and Buick had the GS (Gran Sport).

The owner of the yard had a thing for saving Chevrolets, and this 1969 Camaro RS was saved from being crushed. Its current situation is better, but not great.

TORS

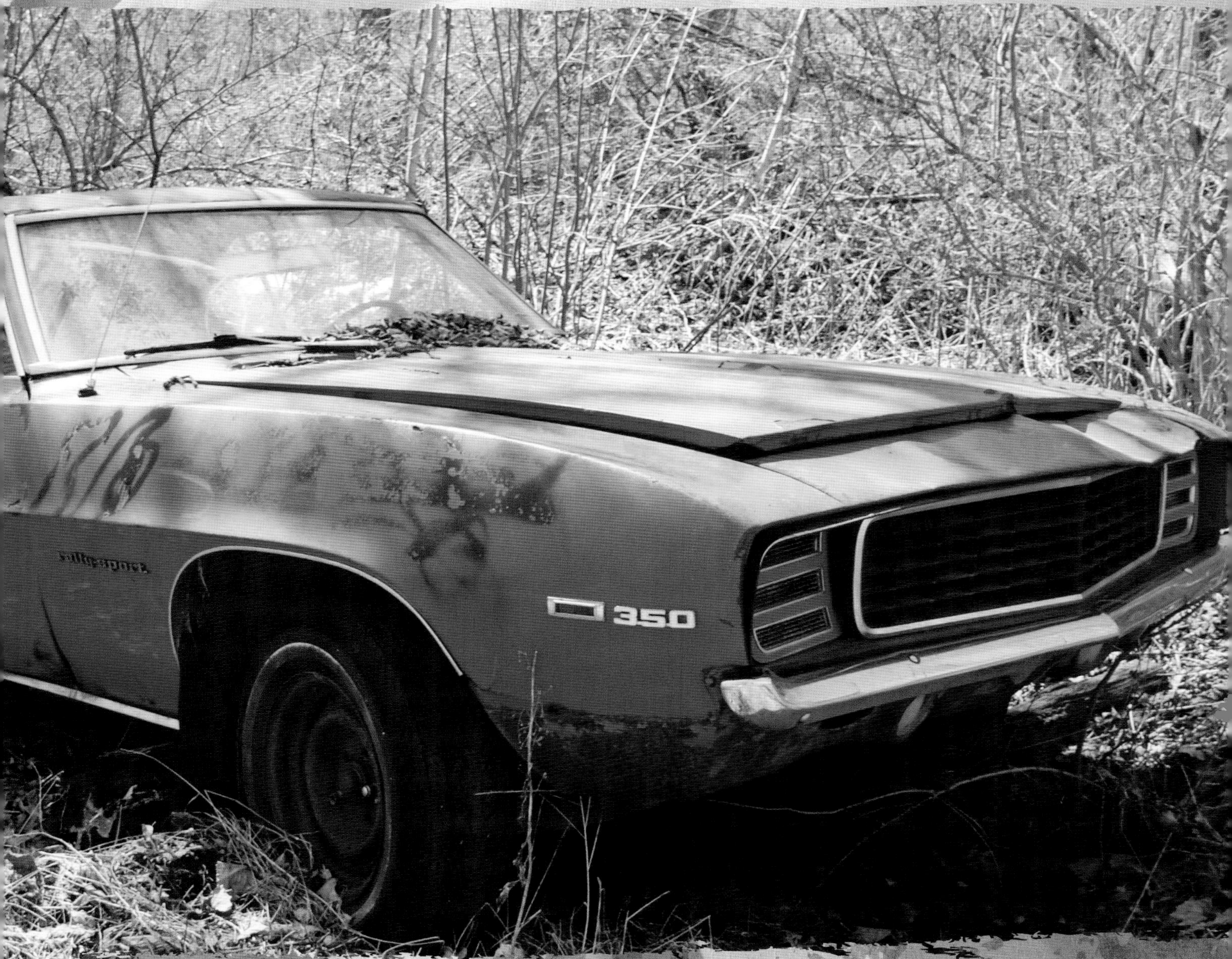

While they were built on the same platform, the GM A-body, they all had different engines during the heyday of the muscle car era. At Chevrolet, the Malibu SS was the top of the heap with the Chevy 327-cubic-inch V-8 under the hood. The Oldsmobile 442 had a 330-cubic-inch V-8, Pontiac had the GTO with the 389, and Buick had the Skylark GS in 1965 with the 401-cubic-inch V-8 (which was publicized as a 400 because GM had a limit on displacement in midsized cars).

Things went well for all parties; the GTO was a huge success and all the subsequent models sold fairly well. Model year 1966 saw the first major redesign of the A-Body since the introduction of the muscle car. The cars became bigger and had more of a Coke bottle look to them rather than the boxy, squared-off look of the earlier models. GM continued producing its full muscle car lineup, and even expanded it as the smaller Chevrolet Chevy II/Nova was coming into its own as a muscle car with a full list of engines and options on the X-platform.

Most of the cars were available with a variety of engines in the early years. The GTO was known for its Tri-Power (three two-barrel carburetors) setups, and Oldsmobile toyed with the setup for a single year. Chevrolet produced a limited-edition Chevelle in 1965 with the 396-cubic-inch V-8. This was the Z16 option and only 200 were produced; the engine would return in regular Chevelle SS models after that.

ABOVE: Of all the cars in this yard, this was the craziest, a 1967 Camaro SS 396 convertible that was sold new by Berger Chevrolet in Grand Rapids, Michigan. It was not one of their high-horsepower offerings, but was a complete surprise to find in a junkyard in the modern era.

OPPOSITE TOP: Buick GS in the 1960s stood for Gran Sport, and this one had the 400-cubic-inch V-8. Being a convertible didn't hurt any either!

OPPOSITE INSET (LEFT TO RIGHT): The start of Buick muscle cars was the Skylark lineup, and this basic Skylark sits in a junkyard slowly being picked away at.

It says Buick GS Stage 1 on the grille, which would be just about the best Buick you could get at the time.

OPPOSITE BOTTOM: While the front half says 442, the main body shows it as just a regular Cutlass, still cool and sad to see, especially sinking into the pond.

ABOVE: Just sitting on the side of the road, this 1966 Chevelle SS 396 has been sitting there as long as I have known about it.

LEFT: Rescued from being junked, this 1970 Chevelle SS is a true SS with telltale signs of being an original LS6 454 car, but sans engine now.

Model year 1967 featured a big change to the muscle car world with the debuts of the Camaro and Firebird. They were specifically designed to be everything a muscle car was intended to be: a smaller body with all engines available, from the inline six-cylinders to the largest V-8's available. All engines were available in these models from the start. The Camaro was available with the 396-cubic-inch V-8 right out the gate in the SS model, and Firebirds were right there with the 400-cubic-inch V-8. They were the cars to have, and first-generation models are among the most desirable muscle cars to this day.

The first major redesign of the A-body and X-body cars from the ground up came in 1968. This major redesign carried on until

ABOVE: The 1969 Buick GS 400 convertible was just about the nicest Buick muscle car you could buy. A truck bedliner stands in for the drop-top on this example!

RIGHT: This 1966 Buick Skylark post car was another resident in the yard. The hardtop version was more common.

1972. All the cars got the new chassis and bodies. They carried on the Coke bottle theme, and you could definitely tell they were an evolution of the brands and cars that had come before. And as before, they all had the ability to hold every engine that GM produced. For the 1970 model year, everything got better as GM dropped the 400-cubic-inch V-8 displacement restriction.

Model year 1970 featured the best of the muscle cars at GM. With the displacement restriction lifted, all the brands went wild dropping in the hottest, largest engines they could with only one caveat: no car could be faster than the Corvette. But some cars got around the restriction, so the horsepower race was open to all without having to bend any rules. Chevrolet put its 454-cubic-inch V-8 under the hood with the potent LS6 option producing 450 bhp. Oldsmobile had its W-30 package 442 with a 455-cubic-inch V-8 with 370 brake horsepower, and Pontiac had its 400-cubic-inch V-8 in Ram Air IV that put out 370 brake horsepower, as well as a 455 HO that produced 360 brake horsepower. Surprisingly, the overall

winner was Buick, as it put the 455-cubic-inch V-8 under the hood. With the Stage 1 package, it supposedly only produced 360 brake horsepower, but made 510 lb-ft of torque and was giving the Hemis the best run for the money.

By 1971, things had cooled down a bit, and the cars were relatively unchanged. Many of the really high-horsepower, special-option cars had been discontinued. All the big engines were still there, but with coming new emission laws and increasing insurance costs, it was the beginning of the end. By 1972, things were on the downswing, and in 1973, the GM A-body had another complete redesign, going bigger and in a more European luxury direction. All the big names still existed: Chevelle SS, GTO, Buick GS Stage 1, 442. But by 1974, they were all disappearing. Some lived on as versions of other models, such as the GTO, which was an option on the 1974 Pontiac Ventura. For the most part, the tire-squealing

INSET (LEFT TO RIGHT): This Corvette is a mostly original 454 car that is being stored in the back of a converted church. The owner used to drive it everywhere, until something went wrong and put it in storage.

Little surprising to find right near the gate of a junkyard, but this is an original 1968 Camaro SS Convertible being used for siding storage. I walked right by it the first time I saw it.

Another poor Buick GN sits patiently in the junkyard atop its brethren, hoping one day to feel the road again.

The crown jewel of the junkyard owner's collection was this nearly all original 1970 ½ Z/28 Camaro, with original LT-1 350 V-8 under the hood.

LEFT: Tucked away in an old horse barn, this 1970 Camaro was quite the discovery along with a plethora of British vehicles and motorcycles.

OPPOSITE TOP: This is one of those mythical cars, an original 1970 Chevelle SS convertible with the 454, sitting in fairly rough shape.

OPPOSITE MIDDLE: A trio of C1 Corvettes keep each other company at a body shop.

OPPOSITE BOTTOM: Now here's something truly rare—a Pontiac Skybird. Basically everything in the car was light blue, even the wheels, grille, bumper, and more. I had never heard of it before finding this one in a junkyard in Michigan!

TOP: While not technically a muscle car, this 1962 Pontiac Tempest Le Mans was the direct predecessor to the GTO.

LEFT: The Bandit would be saddened to see a black, shaker Trans Am sitting with its giant Firebird decal slowly decaying.

BOTTOM: Even sitting in a junkyard, this 1965 GTO looks mean.

OPPOSITE TOP: Not something you come across very often—this 1967 GTO was a surprise to find, especially with a Chevrolet V-8 and dual four-barrel carburetors under the hood.

OPPOSITE MIDDLE: Just down the row from the last 1967 was this 1971 GTO that was in no better shape. It still had a Pontiac V-8 under the rusted hood.

OPPOSITE INSET (LEFT TO RIGHT): Another poor 1967 GTO sits in the junkyard with a Chevrolet small-block under the hood.

 I thought this might have been a rare 1971 GTO Judge, but it turned out to be a standard GTO with the stripes added on. It was still cool to find, though!

muscle cars were gone, but the Camaro and Firebird lived on, adapting to the times.

The 1980s saw a resurgence of the muscle car, and ironically enough, it was led again by Buick, which produced not only a V-8 tire pounder, but also a turbo V-6 called the GN and later GNX. To this day, these are legendary for being insane, all black, and a menace on the streets. That helped lead GM to where we are now, in the full rebirth of the muscle car world with the new Camaros and all the amazing engines and technology that come with it.

INSET (LEFT TO RIGHT): Not something you expect to find in a cow pasture! This white 1969 GTO convertible was in decent condition despite sitting for a decade or two.

Rescued from the crusher, this Endura Bumper 1968 GTO wasn't in terrible shape and the cows in the yard hadn't bothered with the G.O.A.T. yet.

TOP: Not a GTO, but a 1972 Le Mans, this car looked pretty good. Underneath, however, it was pretty rusty. The cows had already knocked off the side view mirror.

RIGHT: The beginning of the breed, this 1964 GTO looks rough, but wasn't in terrible shape with the truck topper protecting the top of the car, and being off the ground helped the bottom!

INSET (LEFT TO RIGHT): Mostly stripped of good bits, this 1965 GTO was in decent shape, for sitting in a junkyard in Michigan for a few decades.

Walked right past this one at first, a 1968 GTO, you can just make out the outline of the GTO badge in the patina on the trunk and quarters of the car.

BOTTOM: I was surprised to find this Cutlass convertible tucked way back in a storage barn at a junkyard in Wisconsin.

LEFT: Just a hulk of a car, this poor 1970 Chevelle SS was once a cool cruiser, but now it is used as a parts car for others in the owner's collection.

MIDDLE: Not one, but two L79 Hi-Po Nova SS cars sit in a horse pasture, where they were parked after being rescued from the crusher. They even come with spare front-end sheet metal.

BOTTOM: This 1970 Camaro SS 350 joined the Novas in the horse pasture after being rescued like all the others.

OPPOSITE TOP: A sharp fastback Oldsmobile Cutlass sits in a junkyard in Michigan, surrounded by other muscle cars of the same era.

OPPOSITE INSET (LEFT TO RIGHT): The Oldsmobile 442 W-30.

Another Olds I had to a double take on, not believing what I was seeing. An original Hurst/Olds sitting in a junkyard, I almost couldn't believe it.

OPPOSITE BOTTOM: I had heard Cosworth Vega models travel in packs, but I had never seen it in person, and I had never seen in person an orange Cosworth Vega before!

TOP: I saw this car for years sitting in this garage. The original owner still has it. It has the Rocket 350 instead of the big 455 because in that year the horsepower was so close, it wasn't worth the extra cash he said!

INSET (LEFT TO RIGHT): This 1967 Chevelle SS 396 has been sitting for over a decade. Once a drag strip terror, it now sits idly while other cars get worked on.

It was a bit surprising to find a mid-'70s 442 just languishing in a guy's front yard, but there it was!

In the late 1970s Hurst/Olds gave the muscle car market a shot in the arm with this car. Sadly, it wasn't meant to be for this one.

BOTTOM: Keeping the cows company, this is another 442 front with Cutlass main body that was saved from getting crushed.

TOP: Nothing but 442 there, and 1970s style all the way around with sidepipes like that. Thankfully they can't hurt any cows.

MIDDLE: This triple green 442 keeps the others company in the cow pasture, I just don't know how someone could get a triple green 442, just not my cup of tea.

RIGHT: Sitting for a while in the same spot, this Cutlass was stuck between a Jeep and a Tree, and neither was giving.

OVER THE YEARS, you hear stories of places like this, but they don't sound real. After all, how could there be buildings full of vintage Chevrolet Corvettes and other highly prized vehicles? I found out while traveling through the Smoky Mountains in eastern Tennessee. I took a small detour and was on the highway to this mystery stash I had heard of. All I had were some clues, not an actual location, about a place on a road and near a town.

Thankfully, it was easy to find with its rows of cars peeking through from behind the roadside hedges. I met up with Sam, the owner of the collection, and his friend, who needed some parts from an old car hanging from the back of a tow truck.

Sam pointed out that the cars in front of his shop were mostly first- and second-generation Corvettes. And parked next to him was one of his major project cars, a genuine 1969 Dodge A12 Super Bee 440-cubic-inch V-8 Six Pack car. Unless you saw the VIN number, nobody could tell what it was, as it was just in primer. But one look at the numbers showed it sure as heck was a legit M-Code, with M meaning the 440 Six Pack option on '69 Super Bees!

And that was just the beginning. Inside a storage room were two 1930s Ford roadsters that weren't in bad shape, but were long-term

This mid-1960s Corvette was without an engine or transmission, or really anything else that matters. But the passenger compartment was being protected by another truck bed liner just to cut down on issues that could occur.

HIGH (ON MUSCLE)

projects. Elsewhere in the room were some Fords, and then the real gold: mostly first-generation Corvettes.

In all my travels, I had never seen such a collection of really early Corvettes. It was incredible. They were three rows of them with three or four cars per row. There were several first-generation Corvettes—a 1954, a 1957 with fuel injection, and more. There was a 1967 Corvette L89 that is an extremely rare model with a unique engine with aluminum heads and a steel block, as well as the Tri-Power—three two-barrel carburetors—on top. There was also a partial 1969 Camaro Z/28, and something completely out of left field: a Hudson Terraplane convertible!

The grounds were littered with cars, including the rusting wreck of a 1969 Chevrolet Chevelle SS convertible, and a few more first-, second-, and third-generation Corvettes, all of them covered in some fashion.

Sam also had a Hudson pickup truck, a really nice, bright yellow 1969 Camaro that he drives to cruise nights, and rows of cars enveloped by thorn bushes so thick you would need a chainsaw to reach the cars.

INSET (LEFT TO RIGHT): 1963 Split Window Corvette, one of the most desirable Corvettes ever, and it sits with its rear end hanging out from underneath what looks to be an old vinyl billboard sign. Thankfully though it protected the inside of the car from the 'elements'.

A nice 1962 Corvette sits half in and half out behind a tarp in the warehouse, trying to keep things a bit more separated. This one was in good condition, and having been safely tucked away for so long, it really didn't need that much. Just to be sorted out and put back together would do wonders for it.

Sitting out in the open for who knows how long, this C1 early Corvette is at least partially covered by the truck bed liner over the open passenger compartment. Thankfully, the owner had plenty of spare parts to put this one back together when needed.

LEFT: This is one of the rarest cars in the whole place, a 1967 Corvette L89. This option gave the 427 engine aluminum heads. And that took about 75 pounds of weight off the front end of the car, and giving it a bit of a performance boost, up to 435 horsepower. This one has been stashed away for a long time, and getting it out would take a long time as well.

TOP: Just about the earliest Corvette that he had in the warehouse was this 1954 model. He had been looking for a 1953 when this one popped up, so he rescued it. Missing some pieces here and there, but mostly complete.

INSET: Another very early Corvette right in the middle of the collection of cars. It was an earlier model, and looked to be around a 1954 Corvette. Thankfully, the car was in a nice, dry environment and not terribly hard to get to, so it was safe and sound.

BOTTOM: Can't get much more iconic then this 1957 Corvette. Black car with white side scoops and a red interior. This was just about the most complete car that was in the building. It looked as though you could just wash the car off and drive it to a car show if you needed to. Unfortunately, it was buried pretty good, along with the rest of them.

In a forest on the property were a few more Corvettes, and a few Mopars, including a 1969 Plymouth Road Runner and a 1968 Plymouth GTX.

A 1969 Hemi Road Runner, a few 1955-1957 Chevrolets, a few first-generation Corvettes, and other oddities were all tucked in a shed. But the top of the sundae for me was the 1970 Plymouth Superbird, which you can see that in the Aero Warriors section of this book.

As I was leaving, Sam said I hadn't seen it all, that I would have to come back again to see some of the really good stuff, and someday I surely will!

IT IS REALLY GREAT TO HAVE FRIENDS
who are as passionate as I am about neglected
cars. In Ohio, my friend Jeff Makovich dropped
me a line about a car I had to come and see: a
genuine 1969 SCCA Trans Am Racer, and not
just any racer, but a Camaro Z/28.

My schedule didn't allow me to visit, until
he dropped the bombshell on me: he had
purchased the car and was moving it in a few
weeks, so if I didn't come then, it would be too
late. With little lead time, I headed to Ohio to
check out this miracle find.

I met up with Jeff and his crew and he led
us to the car's location. As we all pulled up to
the site, I could tell that this was going to be fun
because I saw cars and trucks scattered around
the property.

Denny, the owner, was as excited as we
were. He took us back to the metal barn
where we saw the hulk of the Camaro. It was
a 1969 Chevrolet Camaro Z/28 that had been
purchased new by Ken Stoddart and was raced
for a few years. It was never a road car, and was
always an SCCA racer. The car's paperwork
from the beginning was there, including the
factory diagrams that Stoddart used to convert it
to an SCCA-legal racer. Stoddart drove the car
until around 1974, and then put it away. Denny

The first full view of the car, outside the barn. It looks rougher than the
car really was. It needs some sheetmetal work, but the bones as they say
are good. Frame is solid, the SCCA race parts are still there. This car is
actually going to be full restored.

became friends with Stoddart, they worked together on some projects over the years, and after some horse trading, Denny got the Camaro.

Denny was an engine builder and just-for-fun racer, so the car was put in the barn, where it sat until the day we arrived. The car didn't look like much, and to anyone else who didn't know the history of the car, they would have thought it was just another dirt-track Camaro someone had cut up and abandoned. Thankfully, Denny knew what he had, and was able to share that with Jeff and me.

To remove the car out of its tomb, we had to move all the junk that had built up on and around the car during decades of neglect. While some of Jeff's crew dug into the cleanup work, Denny gave me a tour of the rest of the barn. There was an old Chevrolet pickup truck, a few more cars, and a few older motorcycles; nothing rare or overly desirable, but neat nonetheless.

What really blew me away were the engine and race car parts. There were shelves full of cylinder heads, mostly Chevrolet in origin, and on the floors were engines everywhere: small-block Chevys, a few big-blocks. Whatever Denny could get, he saved and raced, or fixed up and sold. There were also crankshafts, stacks of rims, old race tires, and a wall covered in old headers.

Of the engines, the coolest piece for me was an original Chevrolet W-head 348-cubic-inch V-8 with a triple carburetor setup. Denny said he used to run that engine in his 1957 Chevrolet two-door, which I did not doubt.

Outside the barn was a 1980s C4-style Corvette, nothing that is overly desirable today. But next to that was a different story: the rusting hulk of a 1969 Camaro. It was just a rusty body, but Denny told me it was originally an SS/RS 396-cubic-inch V-8 car, one of the rarest of all Camaros. Unfortunately, this one was beyond help. It was rusted and busted, and there wasn't even a frame to the car, just the body—or what was left of it. Sad to see such a cool car relegated to such a sad future.

Also outside was a neat old Sunbeam Tiger that Denny used in SCCA racing, still in full race car trim. It looked like he had just parked it and walked away a few decades ago. There was another old, first-generation Camaro dirt-track car, again looking like he went racing Friday and parked it Saturday. One fender still had the hand-painted lettering of the pit crew members' names.

But my favorite was his old 1957 Chevrolet two-door, the one that the 348 had come from. At one point, this had been a true hot rod at its finest. Now, its tail abutted a fence and the front end was blocked by a trees growing up in front of it—that's how long the car had been sitting there.

Unburied, the Camaro racer's front wheels would roll, but the rear end was locked up tight. After an hour of slowly pushing and pulling the car down the wet, slippery, and narrow driveway, the car was finally out in the open. It was the first time since the 1970s that it had been out of the barn. The rear end had sat so long, the rims left deep grooves in the dirt—*through* the tires! I had never seen anything like it. Upon closer look, it was bad, but not beyond saving, and all the important original SCCA bits and pieces were there.

We all looked at the car on the trailer for a while, then thanked Denny and headed home. This rescue was unlike anything I had been a part of, and I was glad I made the rushed decision to go do it.

OLDS GOLD

HANGING OUT AT MY CAR CLUB'S monthly meeting, my good friend Carl mentioned that his friend had just bought a car I might be interested in seeing, a 1962 Oldsmobile Jetfire. The car had to be moved ASAP from the garage where it had sat since the 1970s, so I made arrangements to fully document the retrieval.

Their opening the door reminded me of a tomb opening, and as the door creaked open, you couldn't miss the car sitting there in the nearly empty building.

There it sat, on four flat bias ply tires, a nearly all-original 1962 Oldsmobile Jetfire! The car is not well known, and being a 1962 model, it might be a stretch to call it a "muscle car," but I think it is, more than most cars from the era. In 1962, Oldsmobile gave its F-85, two-door A-body platform car an aluminum 215-cubic-inch V-8. This did not set the world on fire, but what made the Jetfire unique was that it was factory turbocharged. Coming out slightly before the Corvair Turbo from Chevrolet, the Jetfire was something else entirely.

Still on the F-85 two-door body, and still having the original aluminum 215 V-8 under the hood, Oldsmobile created a low-pressure turbo to hop up the horsepower. The high-horsepower base F-85 with the same V-8

Walking into the garage, this is how we found the car. I know the owner had cleaned out the garage while preparing to sell the house, but the car was for the most part left alone. And there sat on four extremely old tires was one of the rarest and coolest Oldsmobiles around, a basically all original 1962 Oldsmobile Jetfire.

made 185 horsepower, but with the Jetfire turbo setup, it made 210 horsepower. There were some drawbacks in the program, however. To deal with detonation, Oldsmobile made Jetfire owners pour "Turbo-Rocket" fluid into a container under the hood. It was made of distilled water, methanol, and a lubricant that would prevent detonation.

Unfortunately, no other car on the road needed this, so people would forget to add it. While there was a safety system in place to prevent the turbo from destroying itself if it ran out of fluid, it wasn't the best, and after 1963, Oldsmobile killed the Jetfire, replacing it with a four-barrel carburetor. A year later, the 1964 Pontiac GTO appeared on the new A-body platform, and changed everything.

This Jetfire in the garage looked to be completely stock, with bias ply tires on all four corners, original hubcaps, and the paint looking good. It was a good-looking car, with clean lines and a nice look to the way the front and back ends were shaped.

We popped the trunk open and gazed upon Oldsmobile gold. The trunk was nearly mint, and it didn't look like there was any rust or fatigue. But what was in the trunk is what really stood out: two gallons of original Oldsmobile Turbo-Rocket Fluid with fluid still in the containers. In my research on the car, I had never seen large one-gallon bottles of the fluid. This was like a treasure hunt where we found gold!

It wasn't alone in the trunk, as there were two spare tires and rims in there, which might not seem surprising, but one tire and rim were original to the car—from 1962—and with some cleaning, it would look

Opening up the trunk to the car, we found the original spare tire for the car and a few other bits and pieces. Pulling up on the original trunk mat found a fairly solid trunk floor. But the real treasure was the two original gallons of Oldsmobile Turbo-Rocket fluid!

almost new, it was that nice. Surprisingly, the other one was a snow tire. There were no other snow tires on the car, nor in the garage or thrown away, and it was on the body color rim, so it was a bit of a mystery. But it was fortunate it was there, as it was a rare four-bolt rim, which is hard to come by nowadays.

The interior was just about perfect. We cracked the doors and it looked like it had never been sat in. Other than some fading, dirt, and dust, it was pretty much as it was back in 1962. Usually the cars I have uncovered since the 1970s are full of rodent poop and other debris, but this one had none of it. It was as if someone drove it for a few years and parked it. Another neat feature, which makes it one of two left, is that this car was a four-speed. That's right, a turbo V-8 with a four-speed. I'd call that a muscle car.

The shifter came through the floor and had a small console and boot covering the hole in the floor. Plus, it had something I had never seen before: a Turbo Charger Fluid Injection gauge with two areas, Green/Economy and Red/Power. When you were on the gas, it would move into the Red/Power area, and vice versa for the green. I saw something similar on cars from the '70s called "Economy Gauges," which used vacuum as a reference, but this was unique unto itself.

Once we finally got the hood open, we were greeted again with a time capsule: the aluminum V-8 with a turbo sitting right where it was supposed to be. And from factory pictures I saw online, other than a replacement battery (still from the early 1970s) and a missing "emergency" Turbo-Rocket fluid bottle, it looked completely stock! It was dirty and crusty from age, but everything was there. You could still make out "Rocket Power" on the engine's air intake.

We got the ancient tires to hold air and get the car onto a tow truck. Carl's friend sold it to a gentleman who is THE guy for Jetfires. He had another 1962 Jetfire in the same color combo and everything, except with an automatic. He went through the car and got it running, just in time for the Muscle Car and Corvette Nationals in 2016. It was a huge hit, and now rests comfortably with its twin in Indiana. While I was not able to save the car myself, it makes me happy when a car goes to the right people who will appreciate them.

INSET (LEFT TO RIGHT): That is the nearly completely original Jetfire engine. A few small things were changed from stock, like the battery is a newer style, like 1970 instead of 1962. And the one thing that was completely missing is the emergency bottle of Turbo-Rocket fluid that is usually tucked into the driver side fender support, for those times when you run out!

You open the door and you are looking at the completely original interior for the car. For sitting in a dry and clean environment, with the doors closed and no real sunlight reaching it. The interior is pretty mint. And even rarer, it is a four-speed model, of which only two are known to exist anymore.

One of the gallon jugs of Turbo-Rocket fluid that was in the trunk. It still had fluid in it, that we could assume was the original water, methanol, and turbo lubricant combo. We were just shocked that the container hadn't deteriorated away, or spilled or such. But there it was!

IT ALL STARTED with a 1970 Chevelle SS 454 that is in the Chevrolet section of this book. I know it's funny for a Pontiac story to start that way, but the majority of what happened on this adventure was Pontiac-related. I was contacted by a gentleman who said he had a cool car that was worth a look, and we connected as I drove home after the Woodward Dream Cruise in 2016.

Technically I ended up being there twice. My original plan was for us to meet on my way to the Woodward Dream Cruise, but I got a message that Dodge was unveiling new models and I needed to get to Detroit ASAP. So I rescheduled to meet the owner on my return trip.

And it was absolutely worth it since the day I arrived it was sunny and warm. The Chevelle's owner, who worked for General Motors at the plant where midsized SUVs are produced, led me to the car.

The Chevelle you see in the Chevrolet section is a 1970 Chevrolet Chevelle SS 454. It could be an LS5 or LS6 car, but unfortunately, with no engine or transmission, there isn't a definitive way to determine which. This one had a few signs that indicated it was an original LS6 car, such as an L on the data plate and the larger fuel line, but who knows for sure? After all, it had been rescued from a guy's yard to save it

An old 1969 Firebird that used to run at the drag strip. It was set up with a hot Pontiac engine under the hood, and big tires out back. This car had not been sitting that long, but was neglected, thus the tires go flat and the dust starts to settle on the car.

being crushed, and they had to cut down three trees to get it out!

After we admired his awesome Chevelle, he opened the nearby storage barn, and there were four Pontiacs and a custom car. They weren't your everyday, run of the mill Pontiacs, but were instead high-performance cars. Two were GTOs, and two were Firebirds of different generations.

The one that drew me to it like a moth to a flame was a Matador Red 1969 Pontiac GTO Judge. It was just about the most awesome GTO you could have, and here was one sitting in a barn in Michigan! I could not believe my eyes. It was everything a Judge is supposed to be, with its big, bright red engine, and cool "The Judge" stripe package, a nod to its *Laugh-In* TV show origins, where a character would announce, "Here comes The Judge!"

Starting in 1969 in response to the overwhelming 1968 sales success of the "cheap" muscle car, the Road Runner, Pontiac devised its "The Judge" package. It featured a standard Ram Air III 400-cubic-inch V-8 with some cool graphics and a neat name—and not much else. It sold fairly well, continuing as an option on the GTO until 1971.

The one we were observing was fully loaded, and even had the neat hood tach that they were famous for. The car had been sitting in the barn for so long that the tires had gone flat and started to crumble. The car was mostly intact with all the pieces there except the engine, which had been removed. The interior was there, so it seemed like you could bolt on a single wheel and some new tires and this beautiful car could easily be pounding the streets again!

Nearby was another 1969 GTO, this one was a nicely restored example that looked to have been Verdoro Green. Unfortunately, it hadn't run in two years. There was a really nice 1969 Firebird that the son and father had drag raced for a time. It was a complete car that didn't need much to be running again. The same went for the silver second-generation Firebird we saw. It was also a nice car that didn't need much work to be running again.

We were far from done. We walked next door to the neighbor's storage barn, watched over by the resident guard chicken. Inside the barn was another second-generation Firebird that was by no means perfect, but looked like it was a driver. There was a bit of rust and rot, but it was a white car with tan interior and a black-and-blue Firebird sticker on the hood, and it was still cool.

There was also a 1957 Chevrolet "Shoebox" and a second-generation Camaro. The Shoebox was going to be a serious drag

The nicest car in the barn was a really clean 1969 GTO. This one had been sitting for just over two years. The car just needed some minor work to get back on the road.

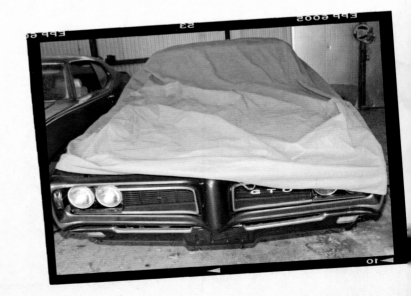

racer as its front end would tilt forward, and it had small wheels up front, large ones in back—the usual drag racing style. It was another one that would be stashed until the time came to work on it.

Heading outside, and past the chicken, we made our way to his father's house, where a large sign on the barn read "THE JUDGE" in the original GTO style.

The father had lots of Pontiac cars and memorabilia, and he was into some serious horsepower. There was a 1965 GTO with a blown Pontiac engine that was totally in keeping with the Pro Street look of the '80s and early '90s. If I saw this thing coming at me, I would move over—and quick. Next to the scary GTO were two more second-generation Firebirds, neither of which looked like they had been sitting much.

With this assortment of Pontiac vehicles to play with, it was no wonder the projects cars needing work were sidelined. I thanked my friend for showing me everything, and I was on my way. It's funny to think that what started with a message about a Chevelle led to one of the best Pontiac finds I had seen.

TOP: The GTO Judge is an original Ram Air engine car, which is the upgraded 400. In Matador Red, this car definitely stands out in a crowd. This one had been sitting so long that the tires have actually started to come apart. Thankfully, the car is in a nice dry storage barn, and being away from direct sunlight helps preserve this cool car.

BOTTOM: Not something you see very often, an original 1969 GTO Judge sitting neglected in a barn. This one had been owned by the same gentleman for a while. The car needed some serious work, so he tucked it away for a rainy day. It didn't help the fact that the engine was out of it, and he had plenty of other Pontiacs with healthy engines in them.

ROYAL PONTIAC

I'M NOT ALONE IN MY PASSION for finding cool old cars in less-than-perfect condition. The current group of such hunters are good friends with whom we can share a unique passion. The guys from the YouTube show *Hot Rod Hunt* travel mostly in the plains west of the Mississippi. Our paths had never crossed in the real world, but we chatted online, helping each other with information on cars we knew about; they specialized in GM products, and it was Mopars for me.

In the summer of 2016, the show's Chris and Rick notified me they were heading to Chicago to pick up a car, and they invited me to come and see the car at that time. I was curious why they were coming all the way from Wyoming to pick up a car, and how did they know about it? It's funny how the universe works sometimes.

At the local car cruise, I learned of a guy named Joe who had once owned a new 1965 Pontiac GTO. In 1968, he sold the car to a neighbor and moved on, but never forgot about that car. A few years ago, Joe chased the car down and was able to purchase it back. He took inventory of the car and realized it was not in the greatest shape, so Rick and Chris snapped it up before Joe could change his mind. And that's what brought them to Chicago!

The original 1965 GTO grille emblem went missing somewhere in the multi-decade slumber, but there is no mistaking that front end. With the bulge hood and stacked headlights. It is a one year only style.

It was great meeting them face to face. I'm normally a crew of one—just me, myself, and I. To have a large group of guys along on an adventure was definitely something different.

We headed to where the GTO was stashed and saw it had been sitting in a garage since 1978. Joe had been pursuing the car for a few years, but the owner didn't want to sell it until she cleaned the garage where it sat. But when her house had to be sold for tax purposes, she sold the car back to Joe.

It took him a day to get the car rolling and over to his garage. When he purchased it, the wheels were flat, the tires ruined, and it didn't help that the brakes were locked up. But by the end of the day, it was safely tucked away in his garage.

He opened his garage door and unveiled the GTO. For sitting in a Chicago garage, it was not in bad shape. The car looked pretty straight, and while there were definitely signs it had been driven, the body was not completely rotted out like so many cars from that era. There was a bit of rust, dents, scratches, etc., but to me, the car had a great patina to it. I personally would just get it running and leave it as is.

Popping the hood, it was all there—well, everything that made this car so special: the 389-cubic-inch V-8 and three two-barrel carburetors. The interior was in really nice shape, so with a little cleaning, it would be perfect; it didn't look as though anything had been eaten by mice or such. The carpet was still nice, but everything was a bit dirty. I wouldn't doubt that all it would need is a good cleaning to be perfect. And it didn't hurt that sticking through the floor was the four-speed manual transmission!

After going around the car and fully documenting it in as-found condition, Joe had another surprise for us: a bunch of original documents from the car. He had everything all the way back to the original warranty book, which was in his dad's name because at the time you had to be 21 years old to sign for it. That wasn't the best part, though. In the piles of paperwork were original documents from Royal Pontiac in Royal Oak, Michigan.

That name might not ring a bell to some, but back in the day, Royal Pontiac was *the* place to go to make your Pontiac fast. They were the Yenko, Nickey, Mr. Norm's of the Pontiac world. Most Pontiac press fleet cars went through Royal Pontiac to be prepped into better-than-perfect condition. They even produced a special GTO called the Royal Bobcat GTO, which was outfitted with all the goodies. The dealership was located right on the epicenter of the street racing scene in Detroit—

OPPOSITE TOP: For sitting in a garage for decades, the 1965 GTO was in remarkably good shape. Very little rust, which is extremely surprising that the car was a Chicago car all its life. It was by no means a perfect car, but the look and patina that the car had, you couldn't duplicate.

BELOW TOP: Unsure of the date, but it is the original owner with the GTO not long after getting the car. These sort of time capsules really allow an individual to look at the history of the car and see that this car was well loved.

BELOW BOTTOM: Paperwork is what really makes the story, and it does not get any better then this. Original invoice for parts and services from the most famous Pontiac dealership in the country. Royal Pontiac in Royal Oaks, Michigan. And time slips from one of the oldest drag strips in the nation, Great Lakes Dragaway in Union Grove, Wisconsin. Which is still there to this day.

ABOVE: The 389 with Tri-Power setup still sits atop the engine, right where it belongs. This one wasn't stock by any means. The owner had hopped up the engine for more power back in the 1960s. One of the popular bolt-on accessories to dress up the engine, still to this day, is a set of M/T (Mickey Thompson) valve covers.

Woodward Avenue. It was *the* place to be for the kids and their cars.

This GTO came not from Royal Pontiac, but from Borg Pontiac in Downers Grove, Illinois. But Joe had the car given the Bobcat kit from Royal Pontiac, and even joined their "racing team." He still had the original "Royal Racing Team" sticker and membership card (for his membership that expired 5-1-66). He had time slips from racing at Great Lakes Dragaway in Union Grove, Wisconsin, and "World Famous" U.S. 30 Drag Strip. This car had every piece of paperwork anyone could imagine, and muscle car people will tell you the more paperwork and history with a car, the more valuable it is.

Joe even had a picture of himself with the car back in the day. It was an amazing experience with an incredible car, and it wasn't the only one in the garage. Joe also had a 1930 Model A tucked away in the garage for a rainy day!

I had to leave before they got the car out of the garage and onto the trailer, but with a crew like Chris's, that would be a piece of cake since the car had been moved recently. I thanked Rick, Chris, and the crew for the opportunity to see such a cool car before it left the area forever. It really was a once-in-a-lifetime opportunity I'll never forget!

CHAPTER 4:
MOPAR

DODGE, PLYMOUTH, AND IN SOME INSTANCES CHRYSLER vehicles—Mopar, as many call it—have a long and storied past within the confines of the muscle car life. Even before the start of what is known as the muscle car era with the 1964 Pontiac GTO, Mopar had a few cars that could easily fit into the small-body, big-engine category, such as the big 331 and 392 Hemi engines being put into the Chryslers at the time. Or in the early 1960s, the biggest, most powerful engines around, the Max Wedge 413 and 426 were between the fenders of the intermediate B-body platform cars. It wasn't until the GTO threw down the gauntlet that things really took off, though.

Playing a little bit of catch-up, Mopar didn't have a direct muscle car competitor. These brands had some cars that could be considered muscle cars, such as the 1964 Plymouth Sport Fury with 426 Wedge engines, or Dodge 330 Max Wedge. But they never took off like the GTO or Mustangs. It wasn't until 1966 that the first true muscle car from Dodge came out in the form of the Dodge Charger. It was a Dodge Coronet for most of the body, but had a fastback rear window. Over at Plymouth, they had their Satellite lineup, which never had a fastback body. These were all great cars, but with their very boxy proportions, they didn't set the sales floor on fire. But they made a name for themselves because they could be optioned with a very unique engine, which some called King Kong because of its awesome power: the 426 Hemi.

A few forlorn 1970s-era 'Cudas were found in a horse pasture. The vibrant AAR stripe can still be seen on this 1970 model.

119

In 1963, Mopar wanted an engine they could put in their cars and go dominate NASCAR, and they gave Tom Hoover the task of developing the engine. They looked through different design standpoints and settled on the hemispherical combustion chamber design that was similar to the style used on what is now known as first-generation Hemi engines from Mopar. His crew took the factory 426 Wedge engine block and adapted a new set of Hemi heads to the engine, creating one of the most feared engines of the muscle car era. It supposedly produced 425 brake horsepower and 490 lb-ft of torque. That was downrated, just like all large muscle car engines at the time, to keep the insurance companies at bay.

The Hemi lived just as the muscle car did: a short and glorious life. It was available in a production car from 1966 through 1971. Few engines were able to keep up with the Hemi, including the Buick 455 Stage 1 cars and 454 LS6 engines from Chevrolet. The one thing they had going for them that the Hemi did not was a much simpler design of the rocker setup in the heads. The Hemis were expensive to produce and had a complex dual-rocker setup. They needed to

INSET (LEFT TO RIGHT): Way back in a friend's backyard sat this Javelin. This one had run and been driven within the past few years, but since then it has just sat back along the fence. With mold growing on its flanks.

Someone needed a half a tail panel from this poor Javelin sitting way back in a Michigan junkyard.

A complete Rambler Marlin sits growing mold on a concrete pad in Wisconsin, waiting for the owner to return.

Tucked away safely in a Michigan barn, this Javelin AMX was the high school car of the owner, and so he slowly works on it, when time allows.

BOTTOM: This original 1974 Javelin with 401 and four-speed that had been sitting in a garage in Illinois for years, pulled out and rescued just before this picture.

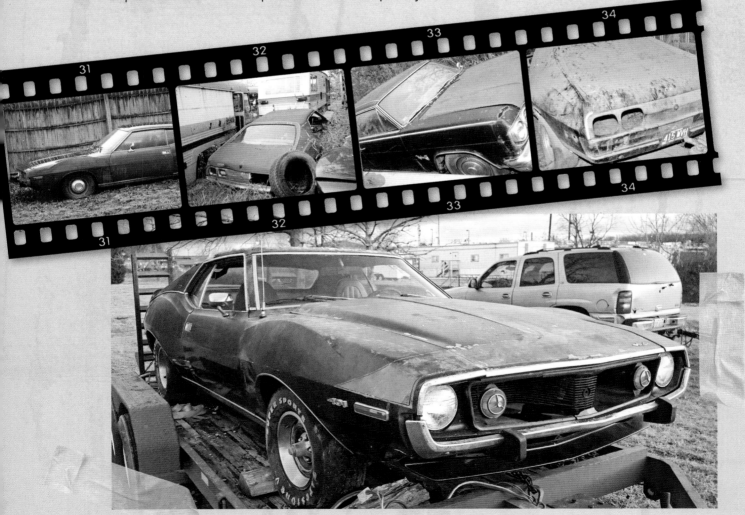

TOP: Another row of AMC products, including a few Javelins and even a Gremlin.

CENTER: This poor Javelin was being used to keep another AMC product off the ground, which did this car no favors.

BOTTOM: You never know what you might find, such as a row of AMC products and some early 80s Chrysler FWD vehicle. The Javelin on top of the yellow Javelin looks to have been someone's fun car at one point.

be properly maintained to keep the Hemi happy, and if the Hemi struggled, the engine suffered. But they ran so well, they created a mystique all to themselves.

While the 1966 and 1967 cars sold well, it was the big design change of 1968 that really made the Dodge and Plymouth vehicles standouts in the field. It led to the creation of one of the most iconic muscle cars ever produced, the 1968–1970 Dodge Charger. With its voluptuous Coke bottle form, large and open grille, and rocket ship taillights, its striking looks sent sales through the roof from previous years. It became both the hero car and villain car in a long slew of famous car movies and shows, including the movies *Bullitt*, *Blade*, and of course, *The Dukes of Hazzard*. It will live on in people's minds for decades as the iconic muscle car of the era.

While Plymouth might not have the most iconic muscle car of all time, they are right up there on the list. They had their own updates with the Satellite lineup and brought back the GTX nameplate from 1967. The GTX was good, having the right muscle car engines—the 440 or 426 Hemi—but it was never a huge seller. Then there was an idea: "How about a low-buck muscle car for the young and hip? Name it after a fast cartoon character." And in a stroke of genius, Plymouth got the rights to produce a car called the Road Runner. It was available in 1968 with just a 383 or Hemi, it was under $3,000, and it was as stripped down as you could get—the exact opposite of the GTX. The Plymouth engineers were even able to get a horn that sounded like the "Beep Beep" of the cartoon character.

The B-body cars were not alone in the muscle car fight, as the smaller A-body platform cars had been competing very well in the same space. The Dodge Dart and Plymouth Barracuda both had a full lineup of engines, especially in their second generation from 1967 through 1969. They were built to directly compete with the

OPPOSITE TOP: I don't know what's worse, the original Levi's Hornet on the bottom being crushed, or the Javelin with the rich patina sitting on top of it.

OPPOSITE CENTER LEFT: The Spirit AMX on top represented the end of the line for the AMX, while below is another 1970s Javelin.

OPPOSITE CENTER RIGHT: A mid-1970s Javelin sits out in the yard in pretty good shape other than the windows not quite sealing the outside world from the interior.

OPPOSITE BOTTOM: Another Javelin SST sits on top of its brethren, trying to keep the rust at bay in a Michigan junkyard.

BOTTOM: One of the craziest things I have seen, a 1970 Dodge Challenger R/T sitting in an old car transport trailer for who knows how long. It looks to have been sitting for quite a while.

Nova SS and Mustangs at the time. Dodge and Plymouth were even able to shoehorn in their biggest engines between the front fenders. It took some inventive engineering, but they did it. But the craziest A-body to be produced came in 1968, and it was never a street-legal car, but was a drag racer only: the 1968 Hemi Super Stock A-bodies. They dropped the 426 Hemi in them and took them drag racing, dominating the field. Sadly, it was a one-year-only model.

By 1970, things were ramping up, rather than slowing down with the introduction of Dodge and Plymouth midsize, purpose-built muscle cars on the E-body platform. On the Plymouths side, they brought over the Barracuda name, and for Dodge they called the car the Challenger. They sold well, but never were the huge success that Mopar hoped for. Even though you could get them with the entire range of engines. After the fact, the Hemi 'Cudas and Challengers on the E-body platform became some of the most desirable and coveted muscle cars in the world. The 1970 convertible versions of both cars, and and the 1971 'Cudas are the most expensive and desirable muscle cars on the planet, regularly selling at auctions in the seven-figure range. While they might not have been a huge sales success originally, they have a legacy all their own.

As 1971 rolled in, the B-body platform got a complete redesign, going with a more fuselage design, that made them looking bigger while in reality they were slightly smaller than the cars before. The full engine lineup was still available, but this was the end of the serious horsepower. Sales dropped for everyone in 1971, and by 1972 the party was basically over. Gone was the 426 Hemi and for the most

Perfect and sad timing, this 1970 Challenger convertible is literally broken in half in the junkyard, but it makes for a nice planter for the purple flowers.

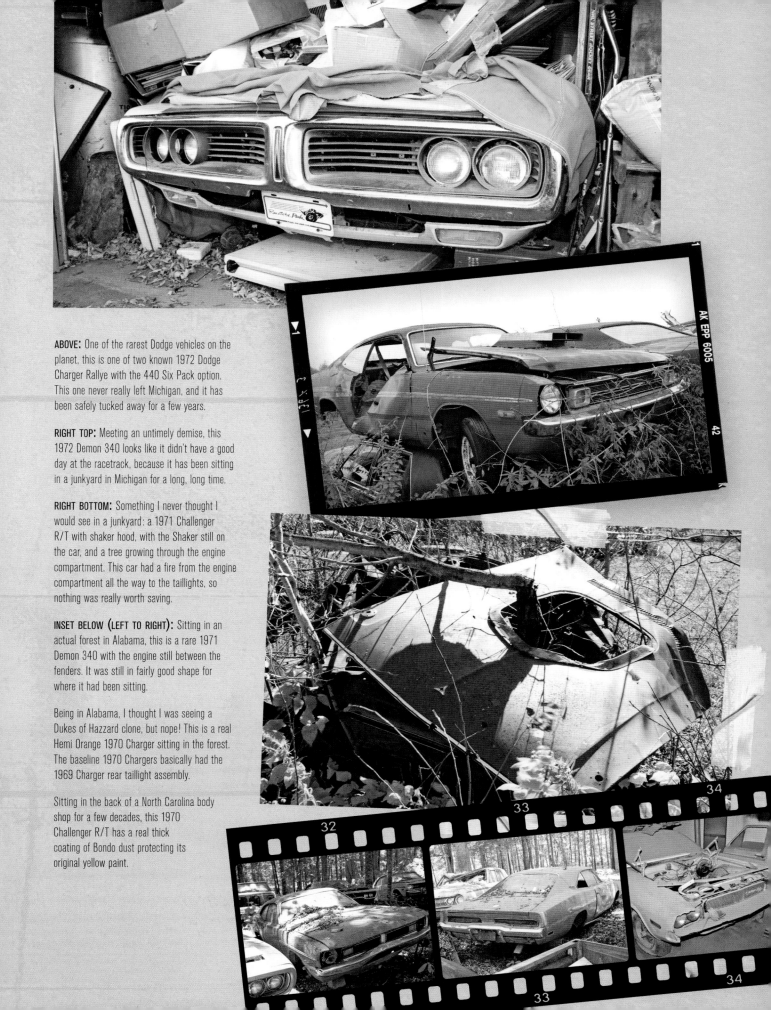

ABOVE: One of the rarest Dodge vehicles on the planet, this is one of two known 1972 Dodge Charger Rallye with the 440 Six Pack option. This one never really left Michigan, and it has been safely tucked away for a few years.

RIGHT TOP: Meeting an untimely demise, this 1972 Demon 340 looks like it didn't have a good day at the racetrack, because it has been sitting in a junkyard in Michigan for a long, long time.

RIGHT BOTTOM: Something I never thought I would see in a junkyard: a 1971 Challenger R/T with shaker hood, with the Shaker still on the car, and a tree growing through the engine compartment. This car had a fire from the engine compartment all the way to the taillights, so nothing was really worth saving.

INSET BELOW (LEFT TO RIGHT): Sitting in an actual forest in Alabama, this is a rare 1971 Demon 340 with the engine still between the fenders. It was still in fairly good shape for where it had been sitting.

Being in Alabama, I thought I was seeing a Dukes of Hazzard clone, but nope! This is a real Hemi Orange 1970 Charger sitting in the forest. The baseline 1970 Chargers basically had the 1969 Charger rear taillight assembly.

Sitting in the back of a North Carolina body shop for a few decades, this 1970 Challenger R/T has a real thick coating of Bondo dust protecting its original yellow paint.

ABOVE: Sitting in the forest in Alabama, this 1971 Road Runner in Violet Purple sits patiently, as it has for years, in the forest.

LEFT: Sitting out back next to a large steel building is this rare 1969 Road Runner convertible, only produced in 1969 and 1970. This one is well beyond help, having broken in half from sitting so long.

BOTTOM: One of the most random finds while driving through Alabama came when I stopped at a small hot rod shop and the owner was kind enough to show me this 1967 Hemi GTX sitting since 1983; he had owned it since 1967.

part the 440 Six Pack engines only made it into three cars before being cancelled as an option. New emission laws and insurance rates strangled the automotive industry. You could still get a Charger with a 440-cubic-inch V-8 after 1972, but it barely had more power than an engine with 100 fewer cubic inches of displacement.

So the cars adapted to the times, becoming more about luxury and cruising. But sales still were not there, and this eventually led to Mopar's first bankruptcy. Completely gone were the gas-guzzling, big Mopar V-8s. In their place were small, four-cylinders that just sipped fuel. There were a few standouts in the crowd, such as a lineup of turbo front-wheel-drive Shelby Chargers and four-door Omnis. But they were not very well received. It wasn't until the revival of the 2004 Dodge Charger and 2008 Dodge Challenger SRT8 that Dodge really got into the muscle car market again. The brand is still there to this day with offerings such as the Challenger SRT Hellcat, the Charger, and Challenger SRT Demon.

It just goes to show that good ideas never die—they just get reborn with more horsepower.

RIGHT: Sitting as a hulk in a junkyard in North Carolina, this is a rare, one-year-only option 1970 AAR (All American Racers) 'Cuda. It has been stripped of almost everything of value and just left to rust in to the ground.

INSET (LEFT TO RIGHT): The owner's first car, a 1969 Road Runner awaits its turn at a restoration in the corner of the storage building.

I completely found this by accident on the side of the road while traveling with *Hot Rod Magazine* writer Thom Taylor: a 1970 GTX sits languishing in Alabama.

Sitting in the front yard of a shop in Indiana is this true 1970 'Cuda 440 six-barrel car with a ton of options, just hanging out until it's brought inside for work to get started.

Photographed just after it was pulled out of the garage, this real 1970 Hemi 'Cuda had just over 68,000 miles and had been sitting since 1976. This thing is so loaded with options that it has two fender tags.

AMC

I LIVE IN CHICAGO, just a stone's throw away from Kenosha, Wisconsin, where American Motors Corp. (AMC) was headquartered and site of their main production factory. That's all mostly gone now, sadly. The old factory site on the lakefront is now occupied by a very nice park and some museums. Most people don't know, however, that AMC had another location where major work was done—in Detroit!

Most people have no idea that AMC had a major base of operations in the Motor City. That's usually seen as the domain of the big three: GM, Ford, and Mopar. But AMC had some styling studios and executive offices not far from downtown Detroit, and this is where my friend Justin comes in.

His grandfather was a head designer for AMC in the late 1960s and 1970s. I didn't know Justin well, but when we were talking once, he told me he had some cool AMC stuff I should check out sometime. I was in Michigan for work in 2016 and arranged to visit him at his house, and I was not prepared for the amazing collection housed there.

As I pulled up, I saw an AMC Javelin AMX in front of the house. Now, I've seen many of these in the past, and this one was not in bad shape. It was white with a tan interior, a cool car, but nothing special. Or so I thought.

When the designer heard that they were going to cancel the Javelin lineup over at AMC, he went and ordered a new white 1974 Javelin AMX and made sure that it was the very last one produced. So that's what the family still has, the very last Javelin AMX produced by AMC. The AMX name would live on, but that was the end of the line for the Javelin name, sadly.

CHAPTER 4

While working for AMC, Justin's grandfather learned Javelin production was ending, so he went out of his way to get the very last one produced—complete with full documentation. You would think he would have ordered every option, every bell and whistle, the biggest engine with the best transmission—but he didn't. It is a 304-cubic-inch V-8 with an automatic on the floor.

That was a pleasant surprise, but not the reason I was there—or thought I was there. We headed to his father-in-law's storage barn and in the corner, in the loft, was the AMC concept car called the Amitron.

The AMC Amitron concept car was designed to be the future. It was an electric car for the city designed to reduce emissions and traffic. It was produced in 1967 as the Amitron, and was redone in 1977 and renamed the Electron to work with AMC's "Concept 80" lineup. But the Amitron was ahead of its time for what it was supposed to be. It was intended to be fully electric, but never got that far. The concept, in all its grandeur, was nothing but a shell made of wood and plastic. The wheels were golf cart tires. It was intended to show what AMC could build if the public wanted it—and the public didn't.

Some Amitron styling was seen in later AMC products such as the Pacer and Gremlin. When the car's usefulness to AMC ended, Justin's grandfather rescued it and tucked it away. It has been tucked away since the 1970s. When Justin had to move it, they had room in the loft, so up it went, safely tucked away where nobody can bother this important piece of history.

Tucked in the very back of a storage barn, up on the storage loft is the AMC factory show car. The AMC Amitron was a factory concept car for an all-electric car. It was intended to showcase what they could do and what shape it would take. Nothing actually developed from it.

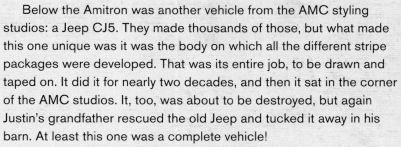

TOP: A better look at the front end of the concept buck. It basically was just safe and dry and out of any real danger. Since the car is nothing but a shell in reality, the buck just needs to be cleaned up to be presentable.

BOTTOM: Before the big concept buck is made, a small one is produced so the designers can show management what they want to do and how it would look. The grandson still had the original design model that was produced for the same car that was sitting in the loft in his barn. How often does that happen?!

Below the Amitron was another vehicle from the AMC styling studios: a Jeep CJ5. They made thousands of those, but what made this one unique was it was the body on which all the different stripe packages were developed. That was its entire job, to be drawn and taped on. It did it for nearly two decades, and then it sat in the corner of the AMC studios. It, too, was about to be destroyed, but again Justin's grandfather rescued the old Jeep and tucked it away in his barn. At least this one was a complete vehicle!

Back in Justin's house we started going through his grandfather's archives, and Justin displayed a prized possession: the model prototype for the Amitron. To sell management on a concept, a small-scale model would be built and presented to the board for approval. These models usually disappeared once the car was produced. Thinking ahead, Justin's grandfather saved the model. What an incredible confluence of luck that both the prototype model and actual concept would end up with the same owner and preserved for decades. It blows my mind.

We looked at all the design sketches his grandfather had created, beautiful artwork from the '60s and '70s showing what people were into at the time. There were folders of stuff that dreams are made of, actual dreams sketched onto a page. I had only seen such artwork online or in exhibits, and to see the actual works in my hands still gives me goose bumps.

We went to Justin's garage to see a few more items from his grandfather, including an all-original military Jeep that his grandfather had saved from being destroyed. It was unique in that it used to sit in the styling studio in Detroit to remind everyone what a Jeep is supposed to look like. It was the purest example of what they were building for the future, and he could not see that history destroyed, so he saved it.

There was also a Model A project of Justin's in the garage, and project scooters and motorcycles. While looking at all the cool projects and petroliana, something on the wall caught my eye. I actually stopped in my tracks—an appropriate choice of words. Before I was a car nut, I loved trains. I still do, and my favorite trains are usually the ones that ran on the Milwaukee Road, especially the famous Hiawatha streamliners of the steam and diesel eras. There, hanging on the wall was the side lettering to a Hiawatha locomotive. I later discovered it was probably originally from a Fairbanks Morse diesel locomotive. Justin said he had heard his grandfather got it when they were scrapping some trains nearby.

The time had come to leave, so I thanked Justin for everything and headed on my way, head spinning while trying to process everything that I had just seen in such a short time.

IN MY ADVENTURES, I've been fortunate to forge friendships with many people around the country. Some of my best friends live states away, and we only see each other once or twice a year on an adventure or two. Other times they end up being in your back yard, and you had no idea.

I met Tommy on the Hot Rod Power Tour a few years ago, and then again in a Hornet Sportabout in the Muscle Car and Corvette Nationals car show in Chicago. I've always been a fan of the American Motors–produced cars, and his was a really nice example. So, we chatted online over time, and he later invited me to Kenosha to show me some of the cool stuff hidden around there. I had no idea he was that close, so I grabbed my friend Bill and we set off to meet Tommy.

Many people don't know that Kenosha was the epicenter for American Motors Corporation (AMC). The company had its corporate headquarters in town, along with multiple production facilities. One of the factories was directly on the lakefront. Unfortunately, AMC was bought out by Chrysler in late 1980s and shortly afterward the main plant was closed, while a few smaller ones remained operational for another decade. The plant on the lake was torn down and the site became the center of

One of my favorite AMC products is the Hornet. This 1971 Hornet was not the high-performance SC/360 model, but the scoop had been added at some point to make it more closely resemble one. It was another car buried in the building, but was complete other than a few missing pieces of trim and headlights.

Kenosha's revival with museums, parks, and even a vintage trolley system that runs in the parks and in part of downtown.

With a long day of adventuring ahead of us, we ate heartily at a true old-school diner in Kenosha called Frank's Diner. A train car turned restaurant, it looked like it had not been updated since the 1950s, and it was the perfect place to start a day of going into barns, fields, and garages.

After a large, greasy breakfast, we headed out with Tommy to his friend's place. I had driven past it for years while exploring the area, but it never stood out. But when you walked into the building, everything changed. It was filled wall to wall with AMC gold.

Joe, the owner of the cars and property, and his son were there working on some projects and were happy to show us around. Most of the cars in the building were not "barn finds" because most of them ran, and had been run recently. Joe had a good grasp of all the rare cars AMC produced, and he had a very nice production 1969 Hurst SC/Rambler in the main garage stall, ready to run out the door if needed. By the front door was an AMC Rebel, a regular Rebel, not the famous "The Machine" Rebel so many people know about. But this one was a factory convertible to which Joe had added many parts of a "The Machine" model, making it cool and unique.

Plus, Joe had a real "The Machine" buried in the corner of the building—and I mean *buried*. At

INSET: The first year for the infamous AMC Gremlin was 1970, and this just happens to be an original 1970 Gremlin sitting out at the AMC farm. The reason this car was saved while so many others were parted out through the years is that 1970 models had numerous unique parts that no other year had, so this one sat as a parts car for a future restoration.

BOTTOM: It's not often that you find an AMC Rebel convertible sitting in an old repair shop, but it also has been converted into a "what if" concept of what a Rebel "The Machine" convertible might look like. It started out as a Rebel SST convertible—which is rare in and of itself—but then having The Machine pieces put on just makes it that much cooler.

My favorite AMC products are the original 1968–1970 AMC AMX 2-seaters. They just ooze cool to me, and this 1970 Model AMX places right up there near the top. This one is buried in another garage that long ago was a small dealership. This one is complete, and if it were unburied and refurbished, I'm sure would be a great cruiser again.

first, I couldn't even tell what the car was until I took a closer look and he pointed out that it was a "Machine." Next to it was something I had never seen before: an AMC Pacer Go-Kart, and Joe had two. Even though one was smashed into small pieces, having two rare karts like that was rather unique.

There was also a nice AMC American two-door in white, and a really clean AMC Hornet. The Hornet has always been an underrated muscle car, but you could get them in the SC/360 model, with hopped-up 360-cubic-inch V-8 that made really fun cars to play with. This was not an SC/360 car, but a more low-line version. Still, Joe had everything needed for a conversion when the time was right.

In this building, the coolest car for me was another AMC American, this one a drag racer. That's not usually my thing, but it was oozing with cool. It had been campaigned seriously when new, so it was fully painted and lettered up, and then the team got a newer car to race and put this one away. For the past 40 years, it sat silently in a garage until Joe acquired it and began to get things rolling. He is going to keep the car as is, but make it a functioning race car again. He was just finishing up on the engine at the time of our visit.

Thinking this was the extent of the collection, I was surprised when Joe offered to take us down the road to his family's farm. It was worth the drive to the property where, painted on the barn door, a large AMC logo was hard to miss. Joe had been cleaning up the property, and what remained were a handful of full-size Ambassadors and a 1970 AMC Gremlin that he kept because of its many one-year-only parts.

Our final stop was Joe's father's storage building. Joe's father opened the door and wow! I know this is going to be a surprise, but: MORE AMC products. There was a neat chopped AMC Pacer on a

RIGHT: Another AMX was out back in the yard. This was a 1969 model in the worst shape of the AMX models hanging around it. But it had one big thing going for it: it was an original "Go Package" car, which means it had a better suspension, bigger engine, and was an all-around upgraded car. So while it was in rough shape, it was definitely worth rescuing.

OPPOSITE TOP: This is an original 1969 Rambler American Post Coupe that was used in drag racing. The car is in original, as-raced condition, having been put away and just abandoned after the team had moved onto another AMC car. So, the new owner bought it and is eventually going to put in a new engine and do some nostalgia drag racing.

OPPOSITE LEFT: The owner's son was walking with us and he knew just about as much as his dad did of the history of the vehicles they owned. This poor mid-1970s Gremlin was going to be his. Yeah, it was missing a bunch of stuff, but he had a dream to make it something. I'm hoping that it comes true!

OPPOSITE RIGHT: A clean 1969 AMC American coupe sits buried in the building. This was the same style of car that was used for the AMC SC/Rambler race cars and factory high-performance cars. Since this one is white, it's not far from being built into a tribute to one of those. It just needs to get dug out.

lift, another one in the corner, even an old cart from the AMC plant with its original paint, which was like the AMC logo! My favorite, though, was the 1970 AMC AMX because I have a serious soft spot for the two-seaters.

The building used to be a dealership a long, LONG time ago, and out back was a large storage area where Joe's family had more vehicles tucked away. Some were nice, others needed work. There was an original 1969 AMC AMX that, when new, had the "Go Package," the highest performance offering for the AMX. But the one that really touched me was a ratty Gremlin in the corner that Joe's son had claimed as his. He and his dad had plans of fixing it up and making it his fun car.

It was a lot to take in, and our group did it in a fairly short amount of time. Sadly, time doesn't stop, and neither did we. But this was about the top of the heap for collections of cool AMC products I have ever had the honor of documenting.

THIS IS ONE OF THOSE STORIES that makes all the time, money, and effort we invest worthwhile. It was an epic find with amazing people and an incredible owner. I just wish it hadn't happened the way it did.

I had known about Terry's stash for a few years, but was never able to locate it. A friend even had pictures of it, but didn't share in order to protect Terry. One day a young woman named Faith posted a photo on Instagram of a blue 1970 Plymouth Superbird that looked as if it had been sitting for a while. She said it had, and that the owner had other stuff lying around as well. I asked her if it was OK to ask the owner to see the cars, and she said the owner would be ecstatic to show me the collection.

Usually in these situations, I don't have to move too fast, as the cars have been sitting for years and they probably weren't going anywhere anytime soon. Sadly, this situation was the complete opposite. Terry, the owner, had been diagnosed with cancer, a rather unpleasant kind. He wasn't doing the greatest, and on a few recommendations, I knew I had to visit him ASAP.

Right after Thanksgiving 2016, I loaded my car and headed south. I joined up with my friend who knew Terry, but didn't realize what

I've found a few 1969.5 A12 440 Six Barrel Superbees in my travels, but never one as complete as this one. Nor have I seen one as complete, and so completely left out in the elements for so long. This poor car was one of Terry's prides and joy, having it for decades. He built a fence around it to keep it safe and near his home.

CHAPTER 4

VERY MERRY MUSCLE

was going on. We met up with Faith and her husband, Jared, and all headed to Terry's house.

Terry had been delayed at an appointment, but he gave us permission to start looking around the outer property. I looked over the fence by his house and there were two very rare Mopars sitting there!

Hidden behind an old wooden fence were two extremely desirable Dodge products, including a 1969 ½ Dodge A12 Super Bee. What made this Super Bee special was that the A12 option package was available for only half a year, and its unique parts were available only for this vehicle and the 1969 ½ Plymouth Road Runner A12. The A12 package included an Edelbrock Six-Pack aluminum intake manifold, three two-barrel carburetors, black steel wheels with chrome lug nuts, and an unmistakable, all-black lift-off fiberglass hood.

This car had been sitting in the yard for so long that moss and mold had taken up residence on the body, but everything of value was there, including the original hood and side scoops, and the interior was mostly intact. The engine was not original, nor did it have the correct Six-Pack intake, but it did have a post-stock setup atop the engine.

Next to the Bee was a Dodge Challenger. It had the 1972-style nose and tail panel, but telltale signs that pointed to it being an earlier car were the earlier-style side marker lights. The car was supposedly built by a big-name West Coast racer, but there was no supporting documentation. It was a complete and cool race car,

INSET: This engine is a Mopar 1969 440-cubic-inch V-8 sitting in a 1969 Dodge Coronet R/T, that is behind a barn on Terry's property. That is not too crazy usually, well at least for me. The really weird thing is what was done to the engine. The exhaust manifolds on the car are off a 1962 Dodge Max Wedge drag racing engine, which is extremely rare. And the intake is the original Six Pack (three two-barrel carburetors) intake and carbs from the A12 Superbee sitting in the front yard. None of it makes sense to me, but it made sense to Terry at some point.

TOP: Terry's main passion was drag racing. He had been doing it all his life. He was able through a series of events to pick up this Dodge Challenger. It was originally a '70 Challenger, then converted into a 1972 style to still be applicable for racing. This car supposedly has a very long history with it supposedly being a Dick Landy car, but there was no evidence at that time that the car had any connection to the drag racing legend.

RIGHT: It took a bit of wiggling through tire racks, but I made my way over to the last car in the barn, a 1968 Dodge Coronet R/T. It was a low miles car, with a four-speed manual transmission. This is about the best picture I could get of the car, and that is of the rear end. The front end was completely buried in boxes and old race car parts.

BELOW: Terry standing next to his Superbird. He had wanted one for the longest time, and was finally able to purchase one. He drove it all over the place for years, even getting Richard Petty from NASCAR fame and an original NASCAR Superbird driver, to sign the nose of the car. The Superbird was an original 440 V-8 with a four-barrel carburetor. It had a few custom touches done before Terry even had it, like the original vinyl top being removed when it was used as a pace car at a local racetrack.

though, that looked as though it had just been driven into the yard and parked.

This was just the beginning. Everywhere we looked there was some interesting piece of a Dodge or Plymouth hanging around. We found rare exhaust manifolds, intakes, Dana 60 rear axle assemblies, and complete bucket seats just lying around the property. There was also some cool cars sitting outside, such as

a 1974 Plymouth Road Runner and a 1967 Dodge Dart. Another vehicle sitting out in the open was a 1969 Dodge Coronet R/T, which is a cool car that was the more expensive big brother to the Super Bee. Same body, but a nicer interior. The R/T was the high-performance model in the Coronet lineup and could have a 440-cubic-inch V-8 or 426 Hemi engine. This one was a 440 car, but when we popped the hood, we got a big surprise!

Indeed, under the hood was a 440 big-block, but the intake was the original Six-Pack setup from the Super Bee sitting near the front of the property. Even weirder were the exhaust manifolds hanging off the heads. These cars had what Dodge called "HP" exhaust manifolds that flowed a bit better then stock. Terry didn't think they were worth it, so he installed a set of extremely rare 1962 Mopar Max Wedge exhaust manifolds. These were the manifolds used on Mopar-built drag racers, and Terry had put them on a 1969 Dodge Coronet R/T that had long been sitting behind a barn. It was mind-boggling.

As we finished with the Coronet, Terry and his friend Penny had arrived and we made our way to the barn. It did not disappoint. You walked in and there was just enough light to see his hidden hoard of cars. There were parts scattered all around—426 Hemi intakes on the shelves, racks of old tires, even a set or two of Mopar Max Wedge Heads sitting in a barrel. But your eyes first went to all the cars.

Front and center was the 1970 Plymouth Superbird that Faith had

This is the 1969 Coronet R/T out back behind the storage barn that Terry had. It is dangerously close to a pretty good fall off as well. It's been back there for decades he said. The R/T option gave you the 440 or 426 Hemi engine. This one had the 440 with all the weird pieces put onto the car for odd reasons. For sitting so long, the car wasn't in terrible shape being in a somewhat protected spot next to the barn, but the moss and mold were starting to take hold.

Buried in the storage barn was an unbelievable find, an original steel nose 1962 Dodge 330 Max Wedge drag car. Terry ran this car for a few years, but for the most part he left the car untouched. The car is still in the original lettering that it had when it raced in the 1960s. And with it all being hand painted on, other than a few stickers, they had a really neat patina to them. At some point it wasn't worth running, as compared to another car he had, so he put it away in the barn.

documented was a real Superbird with a historic past. At one point it served as a pace car for a racetrack, and "The King" of NASCAR, Richard Petty, had signed his name on the car's nose. Originally a yellow car, it had been painted blue for longer than Terry had owned it, and the vinyl top that came on all Superbirds from the factory to cover up shoddy workmanship was removed to make the car look more like actual NASCAR Superbirds, which didn't have vinyl tops.

There was a 1969 Plymouth Barracuda near the door that you could hardly tell was a Barracuda because of all the stuff on top of it. And while the Superbird is my favorite, the neatest car there was the 1962 Dodge 330 two-door, a Max Wedge car with the high-performance 413-cubic-inch V-8. This was the source of the exhaust manifolds on the Coronet behind the building, we believed. It was still painted in its racing livery and had the names of driver Ken Permenter and the car's sponsor, Langley Dodge in Blytheville, Arkansas.

Next to the 330 was another neat car, a 1968 Dodge Coronet R/T with a 440-cubic-inch V-8 and a manual four-speed transmission. It was in good shape and had low miles on the odometer. It was rather hard to get pictures of this one, as the 330 was nearly touching it on the driver's side, and the wall was on the other. It must have taken some real work to get these tucked in.

We went from the barn into the house where Terry regaled us with his adventures from over the decades, including how he worked hard to make his cars fast, how he always did the work needed during the week to get the parts he needed to get faster at the drag strip. He was always running something at the local track, such as his Superbird or even an old limousine. I documented as many stories as I could, and then we all went to dinner in town before splitting up.

Unfortunately, that was the last time I saw Terry. A few short months later the cancer extinguished his bright flame, but I hope his story will live on in the cars and stories he shared with me, and everyone else who listened.

THE DARNED

EVERY FALL FOR THE PAST FEW YEARS, I have headed to the Wellborn Muscle Car Museum to help with a variety of items, and the trip finds me in Detroit before I get home. The 2016 trip ended up being the longest one, at about a month on the road. When traveling south, I always plan different stops en route, and I also try to visit friends who I don't often see often. Sometimes things just work out and I can do both!

Heading south in 2016, I was able to hit up my friend Robert and his wife, Jerri. We had done this before, and always tried to go adventuring toward Alabama, my final destination. Thankfully, Robert had a friend John with an insane collection of cars sitting not far off the beaten path, so after a good breakfast at a neat old restaurant, that's where we headed.

Pulling up to John's place, it was clear we were in the right spot. There were cars scattered around the yard by the barn, and there were horses wandering around the yard. Previously, I had seen cows use a 1969 Dodge Super Bee as a rubbing block, so I was worried about the cars scattered about, but I would learn the horses mostly left the cars alone.

Probably the coolest and my top car on the property was this 1971 Dodge Charger R/T. The car was originally equipped with a 440-cubic-inch V-8 and had the Ramcharger hood option, where a small door would open up with the pull of a handle on the inside. It still had that hood. And even with it sitting in the open field, it was in really good shape. It had not been there that long, but all together the car had been sitting for a while.

BARN DODGES

I was introduced to John and his wife, Sandra, and John noted he used to have many more cars when they lived in Michigan, but had sold most of them when they moved south. What they had now had not been sitting that long, although in some cases it looked like they had been.

The first barn had once been a chicken coop, and it had a weird material on the ground I didn't recognize. We walked in, and as I looked around, I saw rows and rows of cars neatly lined up, with two of John's main projects right up front.

Most of the project cars were Dodge and Plymouth vehicles. Over the years John acquired them from a variety of states. Some were barn finds, others were in junkyards or fields. There were several Road Runners and Super Bees, a GTX, a Coronet R/T, and even a handful of Chevrolets in the first building. I didn't count, but there had to have been at least 30 cars.

The second building was just about as big as the first, and it too was full of all variety of cars, but mostly Dodges and Plymouths. There were a few rare Chevrolets in there, including an Impala SS and a Monte Carlo SS from the '80s. It was neat to see these older farm buildings being used to keep these cool cars in good condition.

Outside where the horses roamed free were cars everywhere—and I do mean everywhere. Between the two storage buildings were a handful of cars, including a 1972 Dodge Polara and some '80s Dodge Diplomat cop cars. Way out back behind the buildings was a random collection of cars, such as a 1971 Plymouth GTX in the weeds with a damaged front end. John had saved the car from getting crushed.

Nearby was a 1972 Dodge Charger with a 1990s Cummins diesel truck engine. Surprisingly, it fit, but it was a beast. John hadn't had it running and had rescued it from the previous owner. There was also a 1969 Plymouth Road Runner and a 1970 Dodge Challenger, but you could hardly see them behind the weeds that were extremely prevalent and tall near the cars.

In the open field was a 1971 Dodge Demon drag car they had rescued. It was complete and in good condition, but needed a bunch of work. It looked like it had been sitting outside for decades before John rescued it. Just beyond that was a nice, clean, yellow 1973 Plymouth Duster.

The two cars just beyond this point really piqued my interest. In this open pasture was a 1971 Dodge Charger R/T. It didn't have an engine, but still had the original Ramcharger hood with a small door

INSET: A 1970 Plymouth 'Cuda outfitted with the 340 engine was one of the best-handling cars of the muscle era. It was very unfortunate to see this one relegated to a field in Alabama.

TOP: A number of cars were scattered around the field. The first one I came across was this 1971 Dodge Demon that had been set up for drag racing.

BELOW RIGHT: Way in the back of the farm field, just edging out the forest sat two more cars. Another 1970 Dodge Coronet and a 1969 Plymouth Road Runner. These were just about the worst cars on the property, and it showed. The Coronet hadn't moved in so long, the weeds were growing up and through the engine compartment with ease.

INSET (LEFT TO RIGHT): I was nice enough to be shown my friends' collection of cars, many of which are sitting in old chicken coops. This is one of my favorites personally, since I love 70 Coronets. It is a 1970 Dodge Coronet R/T. It hadn't had a very easy life, but it really wasn't in terrible shape, even from sitting in the chicken coop for a while. It was actually a nice car underneath that didn't need that much. I actually liked the patina look of the car.

One year older and a slightly different model, this 1969 Dodge Superbee looks to have lead a colorful life. It was in much rougher shape than the 70 Coronet R/T that was in front of it. The fender showed years of battle scars and different color paints. Thankfully, though, it had desirable options, showed the under-hood Ramcharger cold air intake system and side quarter scoops.

Another bevy of decent cars sat inside another chicken coop on the property, including this 1968 Dodge Coronet R/T. This one was nice and dry, with a nice patina. You couldn't tell what the original color was without reading the fender tag. The gray-and-red worn look hid what it was originally. It was mostly complete, though, and safe, so it was in better shape than others around there.

that popped open when a switch was pulled inside the car. It had such a good look that I would have thrown an engine in there and driven it as it was.

Behind that was one of my personal favorites: a 1970 Plymouth 'Cuda. It was originally powered by the 340-cubic-inch V-8 engine, and it had a bit rougher life than most of the others. It actually had some rust and must have been sitting outside for a long time. Mostly complete, it would be a great car to restore. One neat thing about the car wasn't actually anything about the car, but what was on it: the rear license plate frame advertised the Phil Turner dealership, a Chrysler/Dodge/Plymouth/Jeep/AMC dealership in Sylacauga, Alabama. Those didn't exist together like that very long, making the frame a rather neat trinket.

John led us to the other side of the field where we saw a 1969 Chevrolet Chevelle SS 396 by the tree line. And there was a 1970 Dodge Coronet and a 1969 Plymouth Road Runner. Both were in very poor shape, thus their banishment to this remote location. It was still weird to see them in such a unique position, just sitting in a field.

John then showed some of his parts stashes hidden around the property. I know if I had the time, money, and space, I would be just like him. He was kind to allow me and Robert the afternoon to take up his time and show us around, especially with his wife being pregnant at the time. I thanked everyone for their graciousness and hit the road, but I can honestly say I'll never forget his place!

MUSCLE SHOALS HAS
(AND 'CUDAS, CHALLENGERS, AND MORE)

IT'S FUNNY THE WAY THINGS WORK OUT
sometimes. I had talked to Robert online
because at the time he had shared some of my
barn find images with my watermark removed.
We had a discussion about that and ended
up becoming friends. A few weeks later I was
heading south to the Wellborn Muscle Car
Museum for the big Aero Warrior Reunion, and
Robert said I should stop by, that he would show
me some cool stuff. Plans were made and I
headed south.

Usually, people know of one or two cars
in the woods or a field. Not Robert. He was
connected with everyone in a tri-state area! And
he was a diehard Mopar guy, so it was kismet.
We met in town, ate, and talked too long, then
headed out of town a ways.

We pulled up to a nice ranch home in the
country, but there were no rusting cars in the
front yard, nothing to tip me off about what was
to come. We headed down the gravel drive
and Dave, the owner, appeared with the most
vicious-looking little attack wiener dog. If you
didn't give him constant attention or treats, he
would lick you to death.

Dave asked if I wanted to see some of his
nicer cars, and I was all for it. He started pulling

Under the owner's house was another neat storage space. Where the
basement would be, there was another garage. And it was filled with more
Mopars, specifically 1972 'Cudas and a few other project ones. These were
definitely in not the best shape, but being the enclosed basement garage did
keep them dry and safe. I'm sure that eventually they will either be worked on
or traded, because the owner does actually restore his cars one at a time.

GOT THE SWAMPERS

out 1970 and 1971 Plymouth 'Cuda convertibles! He had easy access to three beautifully done convertibles and a Viper, and he pulled them all onto his back lawn. One of the 1971 cars hadn't run in over a year, but he got it running for me to see.

I was flabbergasted to see these beautiful cars running. Usually when we hit up a large barn finds collection, the owner doesn't have a nice car. Dave had a collection of beautiful, running cars, along with a collection of cars that had been sitting for a while. After all the running cars were out, we moved to the first building.

I walked in, and this was more like what I was used to, except for the beautiful 1971 Dodge Challenger 383-cubic-inch V-8 convertible sitting right in front of us. It made me long to have my '71 Challenger finished. But it was everything around the car that was more in my wheelhouse: tons upon tons of cool Mopar muscle car parts.

Various Mopar grilles hung from the rafters, for a 1971 Challenger, 1970 Plymouth Barracuda, 1968 Plymouth GTX, etc. I saw a pile of parts I thought were on a big table or something, but I was incorrect: the parts were sitting on top of a 1970 Plymouth AAR 'Cuda! It was an original dark green car, and its restoration had begun. One quarter had been replaced and parts for it were scattered around the property. Other projects had injected themselves into Dave's production line, so the AAR had been put on the back burner, but not forgotten.

Next to the AAR 'Cuda was what looked to be a 1970 Dodge Challenger T/A! It had the right stripes, but Dave corrected me that it was just a tribute car he had picked up. So it sat while other projects on the list got worked on. Along the wall were rows of Mopar transmissions, as well as just about any other part you could think of. Between the transmissions and the Challenger was a small-block Mopar under a tarp. Dave told me to pull the tarp up, and to my surprise there was an original 340 Six Barrel engine out of the AAR 'Cuda. There also was a nice 1970 Dart Swinger 340 in the garage, but it was a nice running and driving car.

We moved to the house, and if I could have a house, this would be it. It was built into a hillside and had two built-in garages! There was the 2½ car garage on the main floor where a 1971 'Cuda convertible sat, and in the lower basement were even more Mopars, mostly 'Cudas! As you walked in, you saw a yellow 1972 'Cuda, a 1970 Barracuda, and yet another 1970s Barracuda. There was a 1971 Dodge Challenger, but you could see which E-body Mopar Dave favored the most. Also scattered around the lower basement was much of the green AAR 'Cuda from the other building.

And we weren't done! Dave slid open the door to the big building, and the view was jaw-dropping. There was a beautifully restored yellow 1970 Dodge Challenger T/A that was really nice to see, but along the wall was something more my speed: a 1964 Plymouth Fury convertible. This was the roughest car in the bunch, basically just a shell of a car. Next to it was a very nice 1972 'Cuda that was a shelf when not in use. My favorite in the group was the 1970 'Cuda convertible that was an original 340 car, which I feel is the best all-around Mopar you can get, outside of an AAR or Challenger T/A. And next to that was a "what-if" 1970 Challenger T/A convertible Dave built. These last three cars were not "barn finds" as they had not been sitting for years, but judging by the dust covering them, they had sat for quite a while.

There was one last 'Cuda in the building, in Dave's trailer. It wasn't a barn find or any sort of neglected vehicle, but it was something special: a real 1970 Hemi 'Cuda. It had the Hemi under the hood and a shaker through the hood. It was sweet. It nearly identical to the car my father bought new in 1970. That's right, my father bought a Hemi 'Cuda new in 1970, and I still have the engine and transmission. But that's another long story.

Thinking we were done, I was about to head out when Dave stopped me. He took Robert and me out back and in a lean-to was something neat: a low-mile 1978 Dodge Lil' Red Express truck. Tucked away for a rainy day, it was complete and in good shape, other than a broken turn signal in the grille. It looked like you could wash the truck and go for a drive. Things just don't rot away in the south like they do in the north!

Dave had one more interesting tidbit to show: a radio out of 1970s Dodge truck that had a built-in CB radio from the factory. I had never seen anything like it at that point. It was really neat, and it was awesome that Dave had allowed me open access to his collection. And it was incredible that Robert and I were able to enjoy this adventure—and more since—after having a rough start. It just goes to show that most car guys are good guys when you get right down to it!

LEFT: Not knowing what to expect when entering a storage area, this was definitely unexpected, but a true 1970 AAR 'Cuda. This one had a restoration started on the car, as the quarters had been replaced, but other cars had taken up much of the owner's time, and the AAR has sat, being used for a shelf in the meantime. But it is dry and safe, so it isn't degrading anymore.

MIDDLE: In a large steel storage barn were a few more cars stashed away. This poor 1970 'Cuda convertible was a very clean car. Red with a white vinyl top and interior. It was odd though, that it had side impact moldings. Fortunately, the car not being seriously neglected and has a car cover over it normally, until I got there.

RIGHT Out back, behind the storage barn was a lean-to area with a really neat piece of history. A low-mile 1978 Dodge Lil' Red Express truck. This one has been bought and tucked away, knowing that they were only produced for two years. Even with being in the dirt and semi-open environment, it was a very solid vehicle. I was dying to give it a wash and see what it looked like without an inch of dust on it.

THE PENNSYLVANIA

YOU NEVER KNOW WHAT TO EXPECT when going on adventures like I do. Sometimes it is a dead end and nothing pops up. Then there are times like this adventure where they go well beyond your wildest imagination. The cars and their locations are exactly what you think of when it comes to automotive archaeology, especially when the term *barn find* is thrown around. This has some of the best examples of a barn find I have, and it all started online.

You read earlier about Dan and his collection in Pennsylvania. It had been Dodges for the most part before this. The 1969 Daytona in the parts store, which blew my mind, and it was the first thing I saw. It was not the only vehicle though. Next to the Daytona were two 1967 Hemi GTX models. And there was a 1969 Dodge Super Bee A12 440 Six Pack car that had a 361-cubic-inch V-8 under the hood instead of the original 440. That's a rather odd combination in and of itself.

Looking around one room, I could not believe the variety of parts and pieces scattered about. There were additional original 1970 Plymouth Superbird nosecones sitting between cars, and original Superbird and Plymouth 'Cuda shaker hoods stacked in the corner, and a completely restored 426 Hemi, just ready to be dropped in one of the 1967 GTX models sitting there.

Even with a 68 Hemi Superbee in the barn, the hands down coolest car was this 1970 'Cuda. It came with the 340 cubic-inch V-8 and original Moulin Rouge (Pink) paint. This thing you could not miss from a mile away. A very rare color for any Dodge, Plymouth, or Chrysler vehicle period.

It continued downstairs with a mind-boggling variety of rare and desirable parts neatly organized and situated. After that we headed over to his second building in town. It was an older building, and when you are in Pennsylvania, that means something. It was two stories, but built into a hillside, so the top floor was at ground height for that part of the hill, and the lower part exited onto the lower part of the hill. On the building's upper level were two beautifully restored cars under covers: a 1970 Plymouth Hemi Road Runner and a 1970 Plymouth 'Cuda 440 Six Barrel car.

In the bay to the left, tons of fenders and extra parts hung from the wall. The entire wall was lined with fenders from all manner of Mopar muscle cars, and tucked away in the back of the bay was a 1970 Plymouth GTX that had been on a rotisserie for restoration for a few decades.

In another bay was one of the 1970 Plymouth Superbirds featured in the Aero Warriors section of this book, and there was also another 1970 Plymouth 'Cuda tucked away in the corner. At this point, I thought that we had seen it all. Then Dave asked if I wanted to see the "basement." How could there be a basement, I wondered, since we walked in from street level? We walked around the building and down the hill, and then it all made sense.

There was a door in the center of the lower level, and once you opened it and turned on the lights, I felt like Howard Carter discovering the Tomb of King Tutankhamun in Egypt. There were cars everywhere in the basement, every one of them was something. The cars in the basement were tightly packed in to protect them and create maximum space for maximum cars and other items. There were spare doors—rare and unique—scattered about; it made it a bit

The other high-dollar Plymouth in the basement was this non-descript 1970 'Cuda. It fortunately had the R-code in the 5th spot on the VIN, meaning it was an original 1970 Hemi 'Cuda. One of the most desirable muscle cars in the world. This one was missing most of the front-end pieces, but they were not too far away. It was also coated in tractor oil to keep it from rusting.

INSET: Walking into an actual 100-year-old barn just full of Mopars is quite the experience. Just as you walked in, to the left was a 1970 'Cuda. I could not tell anything else, because it was tucked in the corner very tightly. But it had the patina outline of the 'Cuda badge on the tail panel, meaning it could have had anything from a 340 cubic-inch V-8 to a 426 Hemi.

TOP: Way back, in the basement garage of an old warehouse in the hills of Pennsylvania sat this 1970 Plymouth GTX. This was no ordinary GTX, but one that originally came with a 426 Hemi. It had been buried in the very back of the basement, until such time it was ready to be restored. Until that time came, the owner took tractor oil and coated all the surfaces, to keep the car from rusting.

hard to concentrate when Dave started talking about them. In front of the door was a 1969 AMC AMX that was owned by his brother, and next to it was a 1970 Plymouth Barracuda body that was in the process of restoration, or it looked that way from the primer. Of all the cars there, the car sitting in front of the AMX was the one I most wanted to see: a real 1970 Plymouth Hemi 'Cuda. It was missing most of the front-end pieces, but they were probably tucked away in one of the other buildings. Dave knew what he had, and he said it was a Hemi 'Cuda, and I believed him. I wish I could have gotten closer, but unfortunately there was so much stuff in the way, that was impossible. It didn't help that most of the cars in the basement were coated in heavy oil to prevent them from rusting! So they had a rather interesting sheen to them.

Of all the cars he had, 99 percent were either Dodge or Plymouth vehicles. The two outliers were a pair of Mustangs. One was not just any 1970 Ford Mustang, but was a real 1970 Mustang Boss 302! In the back was a 1970 Plymouth GTX, about which Dave said, "Oh, It's just another Hemi GTX." Of course! What was I thinking? Just another Hemi car. Again, I could not get to it, because of the cars closely packed in. But the last two cars in the section were another 1967 Plymouth GTX and a Plymouth Superbird seen in the Aero Warriors section.

That was it, I thought; there weren't any more buildings, from what I could see. Of course, I was wrong. Dave had a family farm with more buildings. The next day, Dave's friend took me over there, and in one building was another fully restored 1967 Hemi GTX. One was originally Dave's father's car, and Dave had the matching one, as well as a long-term project 1970s Barracuda of some form.

Also on the property was a real old barn. So old, you could see the way the timbers had been shaped, and it wasn't done with saws. So it was most likely over 100 years old. It had a lower storage area filled with parts cars or really far-distant projects. Among this group was a wrecked 1970 Plymouth GTX. Dave couldn't let the car get crushed, so he brought it to the farm. There was also a 1970 Plymouth Satellite, a '67 Plymouth Satellite, and a wrecked—now pink—black and yellow 1972 Plymouth Barracuda shell.

Upstairs was the treasure. Time had not been good to the ramp leading to the main floor, as in: it did not exist anymore. We had to walk a plank to get in the door, and with the beautiful Pennsylvania day, it was perfect for what we did next. We went through the door, and there was treasure. Cars everywhere, and they had been there a long time. And as of that moment, there was no way to get them out! So they were literally stuck in the barn. Barn finds as legit as you can get!

In front of the door were a few Dodge Coronets and a Dodge Superbee (a Hemi car, I later learned) I didn't know because I was more concerned with the other cars in the barn. There was a 1970 Plymouth 'Cuda, and a smattering of other vehicles, including a

In the center of the barn was a 1968 Dodge Superbee. I did not think anything of it at the time, the car was missing much of the front sheet metal and there was no engine or transmission. It wasn't a crazy color, so I concentrated on the other vehicles in the barn. That was until the guy pointed out that the car was an original Hemi Car! That made me to an about face and take a much closer look at the derelict shell.

You can see the barn wood is so old, it has shrunk slightly, allowing for light to squeeze in between each slat, giving the area a unique feel. And with being in so many barns, you pick up a thing or two. And the way the beams are cut and put together, means this barn is over 100 years old at least. And the cars sitting in the barn just make it that much more cooler.

special trio of cars. A Mustang in the corner was an early model that supposedly was a very well-optioned car, but the other two drew my gaze. Next to the Mustang was a plain Jane white 1970 Plymouth Barracuda, 318-cubic-inch V-8 car. Just a good, solid cruiser, the kind you rarely see anymore, with everyone turning them into Hemi 'Cuda clones. Next to that was the crown jewel: a legit 1970 Plymouth 'Cuda in Moulin Rouge (pink). It was very well optioned, with road lights, a hockey stripe denoting it was a 340-cubic-inch V-8 car, and the pink color. These are extremely rare to come across, especially in such original shape. My jaw hit the floor when I saw it. It was quite the sight: The barn wood had shrunk over the decades, so little cracks of light seeped in everywhere, and I've never seen a sight quite like that one.

After soaking in the scene as long as I could, I had to head to Carlisle, Pennsylvania, for the annual Chrysler at Carlisle event. I thanked everyone for the amazing opportunity to see such an incredible collection and booked it out of there. Throughout the ride to the show, I went over the previous two days in my mind, trying to rationalize the volume and quality of cars and parts I had just seen. It was so much awesome, with such a nice individual, in such a beautiful part of the country. It stands as one of my favorite adventures ever.

INDEX